T0209034

RADIANT
ACHIEVEMENT

Turn on Your Life, Your Essence,
and Your Soul-Centered Calling

CHRISTINE HOWARD

BALBOA.PRESS
A DIVISION OF HAY HOUSE

Balboa Press books may be ordered through booksellers or by contacting:

Balboa Press
A Division of Hay House
1663 Liberty Drive
Bloomington, IN 47403
www.balboapress.com
844-682-1282

Because of the dynamic nature of the Internet, any web addresses or links contained in this book may have changed since publication and may no longer be valid. The views expressed in this work are solely those of the author and do not necessarily reflect the views of the publisher, and the publisher hereby disclaims any responsibility for them.

The author of this book does not dispense medical advice or prescribe the use of any technique as a form of treatment for physical, emotional, or medical problems without the advice of a physician, either directly or indirectly. The intent of the author is only to offer information of a general nature to help you in your quest for emotional and spiritual well-being. In the event you use any of the information in this book for yourself, which is your constitutional right, the author and the publisher assume no responsibility for your actions.

Any people depicted in stock imagery provided by Getty Images are models, and such images are being used for illustrative purposes only. Certain stock imagery © Getty Images.

Print information available on the last page.

ISBN: 978-1-9822-6561-8 (sc)
ISBN: 978-1-9822-6563-2 (hc)
ISBN: 978-1-9822-6562-5 (e)

Library of Congress Control Number: 2021905022

Balboa Press rev. date: 06/01/2021

CONTENTS

PART 3

Becoming Your Most Radiant Self

FOREWORD

It's time to notice the heart of your callings.
It's time to put your deepest desires into action.
It's time to embrace the powers of radiant achievement.

We need not look far to recognize that a substantial shift is underway—a shift for women to strongly connect with their innate powers, self-worth, and intuition, and to use those powers to guide their life's journey.

Throughout the pages of this inspiring book you will discover the significance of your soul callings, dreams, and desires and how they impact a fulfilling life. Christine has beautifully defined the path to RADIANT ACHIEVEMENT, sharing inspiring examples and practices that will lead you to design and live your calling, authentically and unapologetically.

When you master the foundational powers outlined in this book, you will embrace an achievement model that is sourced from the inside out. You'll find ways to create a journey full of positive energy, joy, and growth. And, more than ever, you'll see yourself as a leader who owns her gifts to positively impact the world.

Marsh Engle
#1 Bestselling Author
Lead. Amazing Woman. Lead
Founder of Amazing Woman Nation

THIS BOOK HAS SPECIAL BONUS FEATURES!

 Get the *"Radiant Achiever"* App
In iPhone / Android App Stores

This FREE app allows you to access bonus content created for each of the chapters. Simply download the app and enter the special code at the end of each chapter (on the TRACK NOW screen) to access that specific content.

DEDICATION

This book is dedicated to all my sisters—to my natural sisters, to my sisters-in-law, and especially to the amazing, courageous, beautiful women who have become part of my soul-sister tribe. You inspire and motivate me every day to shine my light of love, hope, and inspiration!

And most importantly, this book is dedicated to EVERY woman who has ever:

- felt like she wasn't enough;
- dimmed her light for one reason or another;
- lived from her head, ignoring her heart and intuition;
- doubted her ideas, gifts, and talents and spent any time thinking they were not important;
- gone through the motions of life, feeling numb and disconnected from her beautiful essence;
- felt like she had to apologize for being herself and for the goals she desired to achieve.

This book was written for YOU!

ACKNOWLEDGMENTS

I acknowledge my children, parents, family, and soul sisters for their support and encouragement as I brought one of my soul callings to life with the writing of this book.

Additionally, I warmly acknowledge all my coaches, mentors, teachers, and business associates. You took me under your wings, shared your wisdom, listened with an open heart, and supported me to reconnect with my radiance, find my voice, and shine my light in ways I never thought possible.

And one final person I acknowledge—my true, authentic self. Thank you for always being with me, even when I couldn't see you due to the stories I'd made up about you. Thank you for gently showing me more and more of yourself and the possibility you hold. I am deeply grateful and touched by your love and beauty, and I pray this book does justice to the amazing woman you are.

ADVANCE PRAISE FOR RADIANT ACHIEVEMENT

Christine dedicates this book to all women who struggle with emotions of "not enough-ness," who have led their lives not listening to their inner desires and are ready to make a shift. This book was written for me! I want to thank Christine for writing to us, for putting the message out there that it is never too late to find your own powers, confidence, and beauty within.

This book has encouraged me to take action on a dream I wanted to pursue, but where the chaos and conflicting voices in my mind made me freeze in the process. Radiant Achievement *is a clear, step-by-step guide with powerful messages and exercises to reflect on. It will get you out of your rut and into a mindset of belief and action to work towards creating YOUR STORY.*

Judy Loe
Owner, Thrive With Judy

Christine has beautifully tapped into her inner wisdom and created a masterful guide (or approach) that delicately challenges us to search for our deepest desires. She provides practical and meaningful tips to help us see how we can achieve our dreams and goals. Her examples are relatable for us to SEE exactly where we might begin reflecting and transitioning in becoming our most radiant self!

I have been blessed to personally watch Christine blossom into her awakenings and attest that her passion and energy for life are genuine and inspiring! She helps everyone she comes in contact with to understand—we are all beautiful, perfect human beings!

Judy Michell

Former Human Resources Director

Christine's passion for helping women to find their souls' calling "radiates" throughout this entire book! She guides us through a clear seven-step approach to help us get out of our heads and connect to our hearts, which is where the magic happens. This book is a perfect read for anyone looking to stop <u>pushing</u> for results and to start <u>allowing</u> the beautiful process to unfold with joy and ease. I highly recommend it!

Tambra Wayne

Founder, Om Matters

Radiant Achievement *is an extraordinary book that taps into our very own essence and how we ourselves can use this to our very best advantage to fully be and experience ourselves in our ultimate capacity and beyond.*

Christine Howard so beautifully explains within each chapter all the different stages of being and becoming Radiant with detailed descriptions followed with tools to help one understand and achieve all of the different radiant powers that are in all of us. In Radiant Achievement *she shares how she has grown and is a true example to all of us how we can overcome difficult times and grow from them in ways we couldn't have imagined with our Radiant Powers. We owe it to ourselves to read her book and follow Christine's Radiant Powers, as it is such a beautiful way to live.*

Lisa McCallum

Owner, LisaMcCallumTalks.com

Christine's transparency and courage to share her experiences and lessons are truly inspiring. I love how she empowers the reader to dive back into her innate power and unleash it with the guidance of Radiant Achievement! *The questions at the end of each chapter encouraged me to really sit and reflect on my own story, experiences, and the lessons that I have learned along my own journey. Her story and powerful thoughts and ideas around how we can rise back up and start to live our true, authentic lives is definitely worth sharing!*

Thank you, Christine, for your wisdom and guidance.

Angelic Ingram
Founder, A Mindful Journey to Freedom

Before reading Radiant Achievement, *I considered myself a failed over-achiever. I always had ideas and several projects going at once. My goals in life never seemed to be enough, and I didn't feel fulfilled in the achievements I had made. Christine guided me to understanding that I had been externally seeking a sense of accomplishment for things that didn't even speak to my heart.*

When I implemented the core powers of Radiant Achievement, *I felt a new level of fulfillment in my life. Particularly, the powers of Inner Listening, Reflection, and Rituals helped me develop the process and gave me the space I needed to hear what I needed for myself. I'm excited to see where this new model of achievement will take me.*

Estee Gubbay
Owner, Luxurist Travel Agency

INTRODUCTION

If you've picked up this book, I am guessing you are someone who has a healthy dose of ambition and might even describe yourself as a masterful achiever. While you may be achieving a lot in your life, you may also be feeling overworked, exhausted, and a bit depleted from constantly striving and pushing to have, do, and be more.

Or are you a different type of achiever—a nurturing achiever who is there for everyone else—for her kids, her significant other, her family, and her boss or company? Do you love to help and support others to reach their goals and dreams, but you don't do the same for yourself? If so, you may feel unappreciated, resentful, and honestly, unfulfilled. In the rare case when you do something for yourself, do you feel guilty for taking time away from serving others and find yourself apologizing for what you want?

Then again, you just might be the inspired achiever who now faces life alone or with a lot more freedom as the result of a major life transition such as divorce, a health crisis, or an empty nest. That kind of transition leaves us questioning life and how we will move on in this new phase that is different from what has been before. Are you thinking this time is for you, but it's been so long since you did something for yourself that you doubt you can achieve what now calls you?

Maybe you are like I was, a differing blend of each of these characters at different points in life. The common thread with these different achievers is an underlying feeling of disconnection from some deeper part of self—the part that contains our unanswered callings. We are proud of all that we have accomplished, but find ourselves asking, "Is this all there is? What does true fulfillment look and feel like?"

These thought patterns ran subconsciously in my head for years, until it all bubbled to the surface of my life in unexpected ways. This book tells of my journey to answer these questions, the wisdom I gained, and my new approach to achievement that developed as a result of things "bubbling up." Before I reveal what you'll learn in this book, let me share a bit of my journey that led me to discover the amazing, energizing, path of achievement—Radiant Achievement. What started as a term to help me explain my inner and outer shifts has now become one of my life mantras. Mantras are words, formulas, or phrases we repeat frequently, that often become true.

Radiant Achievement stems from my life path as a young girl—it was how I naturally approached achievement in my youth. Owning my worth and listening to my intuition, bringing my inspired ideas to life—that's who I innately was. As a young adult, I connected with and honored my callings to move across the country (heading west twice), to trade my corporate career for my soul calling as a coach, and to compete in fitness and figure competitions. However, somewhere in the process of becoming a wife, mother, and home-based business owner, I slipped into the unconscious, conditioned trap of needing approval from others, not believing I was enough, and denying my own Radiance. Each year of living this way took a bigger and bigger toll on me. My downward spiral of self-denial culminated in breast cancer and the end of my marriage. These jolting events awakened and inspired me to reconnect with my true essence, to honor my callings, and to rise in my Radiance. The changes and resulting joy, peace, and fulfillment have been astounding.

I am a walking, breathing, living testimony to the transformative power of Radiant Achievement. Now at age 58, I feel younger, happier, more hopeful, energetic, and excited for my life. I feel there is truly no limit to the happiness and fulfillment that is possible. I have a deep trust in myself and my journey. Living with this deep trust has brought me peace. I've enjoyed many synchronistic and serendipitous moments that have made me laugh and viscerally get that all of life is organizing around my success. I have been gifted an entirely new life, not by magic or luck, but by an openness and willingness to live from the inside out.

A radiant, turned-on life awaits when you
step into Radiant Achievement.

Radiant Achievement is an approach to achievement that shifts us from frenzy to flow and leads to a beautiful, radiant, turned-on life. It is a natural eco-system where our core inner powers work synergistically to support us in reaching our highest levels of achievement, joy, and fulfillment. This rebirth and reorientation to achievement can be applied to our interactions with every facet of life—how we live, lead, and achieve. What unfolds then is an opening and expansion of a life that is authentic, wholehearted, trusted and at ease as we see our true essence more and more in everything we do.

Living, leading, and achieving using the powers of Radiant Achievement as outlined in this book will transform your life. You cannot help but be transformed when you understand and engage your Powers of Radiant Achievement. It is a natural byproduct of the work! This book can awaken your radiant turned-on life. Here's what you can expect to see and experience:

Internally

- You feel a deep love and appreciation for who YOU uniquely are; you feel your worthiness.
- You engage your intuition, you hear your inner guidance, and you are confident to take action.
- You become keenly aware of the thoughts you think and can consciously shift your mindset and thoughts to ones that empower you.

- You become connected with your unique purpose and callings and how to express that, regardless of your current career.
- You are genuinely more grateful, joyful, loving, and peaceful.
- You expand your ability to receive.
- You experience joy, ease, flow, peace, fun, and synchronicities that make you laugh.
- You are aligned with your essence, and you are aligned with your truth.
- You are deeply committed to yourself to bring your innate desires to life.

Externally

- You have better relationships with stronger communication, trust, and freedom.
- You confidently speak your truth and ask for what you desire.
- You set healthy boundaries.
- You understand and accept others for where they are in their journey.
- You have more energy.
- You experience ease and flow, and your goals manifest with less effort.
- You bring to life your deepest callings, dreams, and desires.

All these results equate to what you may secretly long for—the freedom to express yourself authentically, to wholeheartedly pursue goals, dreams, desires, and callings that are important to you, to love and appreciate who you are, and to live a fulfilling life.

If you desire to ignite a radiant, turned-on life,
look at how you approach achievement.

This book is not just theory. It contains a deep wisdom that you may have forgotten, deep wisdom that sits inside you waiting to be reignited. Instead of looking externally for things to change, realize that you are the master of your life. You are at the wheel, and change will only come when you begin to live differently. I propose that the time is now, my dear friend. If you are overwhelmed, overworked, stuck, not owning your worth, looking externally for fulfillment, wait no longer. In order for things to change, YOU must change. As you've likely heard, "If you continue to do what you have always done, you will continue to get what you have always gotten." Only you can decide where you are on the spectrum of frustration, suffering, and denial of your true self and inner callings. Any delay is another day of suffering for you, whether silently or out loud. If more suffering doesn't appeal to you, then it's time to get off the hamster wheel of the status quo.

My dear friend, living a more radiant and fulfilling life is your birthright. It is all possible for you if you only commit to it. Commit by taking a journey with me in the pages ahead. Here you will learn a new way to empower your life and achieve your deepest desires. In Part 1, you will learn why we need a new approach to achievement and what the new approach is. Part 2 introduces you to each of the seven Powers of Radiant Achievement. I'll define each power and why it's important to Radiant Achievement. You'll hear stories of my life before I adopted the power and how my life transformed after embodying the power. At the end of each power chapter, you will find tools to connect with and expand your Powers of Radiant Achievement starting now. The last section, Part 3, shows how to apply the powers to how you lead and how you live your life. It offers an assessment to see how engaged the powers are in your life right now, and it identifies your next steps for further implementation.

By the end of the book, it is my intention that you:

- see and connect with the Radiance you already possess;
- understand how Radiant Achievement supports your living a radiantly fulfilling, turned-on life;

- see how you can use Radiant Achievement in your personal life and as a leader;
- understand each of the Powers of Radiant Achievement and your ability to activate and use these powers for your benefit;
- reach clarity and movement in the next steps that support your achievement of goals, dreams, and soul-centered calling;
- have access to support in developing your plan to further integrate these powers.

If you are an achiever like me, you may feel tempted to skip to the end of the book to see how to put it all into action. Hold tight, because every chapter is filled with a radiant ignitor, ways you can uncover, unlock, and reveal your powers that have likely gone overlooked for too long. Read through Part I fully before you explore Part 2 and Part 3. In Part 2, feel free to explore the powers in the order you feel most drawn to read—but do read them all. If you feel compelled to skip a power or deem it unimportant, that is meaningful information to consider when you read that chapter.

Let's dive deep into a new way of living and achieving that awakens your Radiance and shines it on your life and the lives of everyone you touch. Together we will ignite your turned-on life, connect with your true essence, and bring to life your soul-centered calling.

PART 1

The New Paradigm
for Achievement

The time has come to stop living by our conditioning and to step into new ways of being that support the expression of our highest potentials.

CHAPTER 1

The Need for A Soul-Centered Style of Achievement

Women are finding the traditional, strategic model of achievement to be outdated.

The new and necessary way of achieving accesses women's inner Powers of Radiant Achievement.

There is no denying it, we live in a do, do, do, success and achievement-oriented society. The more we have on our plates, the bigger the accolades from family, friends, and especially our culture. We've developed an I CAN DO IT attitude that has an undercurrent of *I can do it all by myself.* To get more done, we tell ourselves we just need to be more organized and have better plans. Committing to do that, we say yes with our mind, even when our heart is saying no. We say yes to our boss to pick up the additional project, we say yes to our child to volunteer for the after-school committee, and we say yes to that friend to whom we are "in debt."

By the end of the week, we wonder what's happened to our life. We are exhausted, overworked, disconnected from what makes us happy; and worst of all, we feel sad that we don't have time to do the things WE really want to do, like take that art class, dance lesson, or trip. Days, weeks, and months pass by. While we get things done, we feel a growing disconnect and discontentment. Is this all there is? Is this what my life is about?

Here's how it played out for me. Year after year, I ignored pursuing my yearnings, my inner callings. These callings were of all types and sizes, such as a call to create new family traditions, a call to do service in my community, a call to learn how to ballroom dance, and a call for solo family vacations. None of my callings screamed "save the world," but they might as well have been that big, given how I felt about them in the moment. In all of these cases, I let someone else's voice, idea, or opinion override my heart. Little by little, I began to give up on me.

By the time I turned fifty, I dimmed myself down so much that I became disengaged from my true essence and innate powers. I transformed into someone who used logic and planning to identify, pursue, and achieve her goals, to run the home, my business, and my key relationship. Getting really good using my inner performing qualities, I spent a large stretch of my life living mostly from my head. I became a systematic achiever. This took a huge toll on me. I became a shell of a woman, feeling dull, unattractive, and honestly, lifeless.

The problem with this is that while we are accomplishing things in the material (physical) world, we are doing so without connecting to our inner worth, wisdom, and creativity. The problem further becomes one of striving and pushing to achieve our goals. When we finally "make it," many of us realize that we were pushing and striving for things that ultimately didn't matter.

What is achievement, really? Let's break it down into some common elements and terms. To keep things simple, I will use the word *goal* interchangeably for goals, dreams, intentions, desires, and callings. Callings and desires are deeper yearnings that seem to be a part of you. You have not done anything special to "get" these desires or callings, they are simply there. Desires and callings can be clarified into one or more dreams or intentions, and our dreams and intentions may be broken into smaller goals. Regardless of how big or small you choose to focus, you will ultimately be working toward the achievement of SOMETHING. In this book, that something is referred to as your goal.

To further set the stage, let's all get on the same page regarding achievement and achieving. Here's how Dictionary.com defines *achievement*:

1. something accomplished, especially by superior ability, special effort, great courage, etc.; a great or heroic deed
2. the act of achieving; attainment or accomplishment

Reading this definition leads us to the word *achieving*:

1. to bring to a successful end; carry through; accomplish
2. to get or attain by effort; gain; obtain

Achievement is all about accomplishing something, attaining your goal, bringing your goal to a successful end. Sounds pretty good, right? Isn't that the intention of all our goals? To actually see them manifested in the world? To see them become a reality? Why would we set a goal if we didn't intend to accomplish it?

I love setting and achieving goals, I always have. Just thinking about achieving a dream gets me excited. I have been setting and achieving goals my entire life. Some I created and pursued through a strategic model, and others I created and pursued with the approach of Radiant Achievement.

> **When we know the core elements of achievement, we are already on our way to Radiant Achievement.**

I have found that the achievement process for any goal contains four main components. The first is **identifying the goal** (i.e., clarifying what you want to do); secondly, **how you go about achieving the goal** (the method, system, steps you use); third, **what you actually accomplish**; and lastly, there is **the impact of your achievement** (on yourself, others, and the world).

Regardless of whether you write down your goals or whether you use the forever popular S.M.A.R.T. method (specific, measurable, attainable, relevant, time-based), or you just have a gut feeling of what you desire to accomplish, your achievement will ultimately connect with each of these four elements. You have control over the first three components, as they represent your choices. While you have the power to influence the impact of your goal, that tends to be a bit more out of your hands, and you may never realize the full impact of your achievement in your lifetime. The ripple effect of what we do is immeasurable. This is important to keep in mind as we move through the rest of the book.

Is it possible that Systematic Achievement is limiting our potential?

Now that I've set the stage for achievement, let me define the existing model of achievement as I've previously experienced it and how I have seen many others experience it. For the fun of it, I'm going to call this old model *systematic achievement*. While this model has positive points, I will focus on the aspects that make it limited and obsolete in our changing times of more consciousness. I encourage you to put yourself in these scenarios and see which ones demonstrate how you've been handling your own achievement.

In the systematic achievement model, the first weak point appears in identification of the goal. Culturally we are taught that we can achieve anything we set our mind to. Conceptually, this sounds good; but in reality, I have seen myself, clients, and many other people set a goal in this very common way: **from the outside in**! Have you ever done this—looked externally to decide what your goals, dreams, and desires should be? We look at our friends, business associates, or even celebrities and popular Instagram and YouTube influencers to see what they are up to. If they are doing it, maybe we should too! So, we set a goal based on what others are doing. We can justify it logically, but chances are we are not connected to it internally. This outside-in approach sets us up for struggle and potential failure.

One way this played out for me was in my coaching business. At one point, my business goals were overly focused on what the gurus told me versus what my intuition told me. One key example from early in my business that created a lot of struggle and frustration for me was when I made income goals my first priority. I was told that was the right way to go if I wanted to be successful. For several months in a row, I did my best to follow my then-coach's instructions. I created spreadsheets that broke my income down by service provided and how many of each I needed to sell to hit my goal. From there, I hustled and pushed to make things happen. I plotted, strategized, and worked myself into a ball of anxiety as each day ticked along. After several months of this, I gave up on the goal and the approach. I was tired of focusing only on the number and of beating myself up for failing at what I had been taught.

My second type of strategic approach—one that I had a lot of experience with before my awakening—was to create goals based on **what others wanted** me to do. That included my spouse, children, and other family members. Have you ever committed to a goal because you felt you had to or should? This is another example of goal setting from the outside in. If you have ever set a goal this way, how did it work out for you? Did you pursue it half-heartedly, struggling to take actions due to a lack of motivation? Or, if you are a type-A personality, did you pursue it at all costs?

This approach, like the prior one, sets us up for struggle and potential failure, because we have little or no internal connection with it. I spent numerous hectic years feeling like I was on a treadmill going faster and faster every year. I got a lot done, but by the end of the year I felt sad and unfulfilled. One especially difficult goal I pursued was a kitchen remodel in one of my houses. My husband at the time wanted to "just do it," but as the person who paid the bills and managed the home finances, I didn't see that as a smart way to handle the project. Already facing a large college tuition bill, I felt conservative about the money for this project. I intended to measure twice and cut once, as the cost to redo is expensive.

I was still gathering quotes to finalize the plans before we committed to the full-scale project when I arrived home one morning after a workout. I walked in the door right as my then-husband and father-in-law were taking sledgehammers to my kitchen walls. My jaw dropped when I heard a synchronized whack. My heart sank even further when my husband said, "I figured the project would never get started if I had to wait for you. So, I just started it." My hurt went deep. Talk about a disconnect in perspectives and beliefs.

Here's how this scenario ultimately played out for me. Faced with a crumbling kitchen, I had no time to sulk. I did what I had done for many other projects and events that were dropped in my lap. If I wanted a say in how things turned out, I had to suck it up and be part of the project on the fly. As typically happened, I quickly became the project manager and broke into DO mode. I focused on staying one step ahead of my husband. Talk about stressful! I did complete the project in time for my daughter's high school graduation, but I was burnt out, tired, and frustrated when it was all said and done. The kitchen looked beautiful on the outside. Inside me, I felt depleted.

> *When you approach your goal with only your mind,*
> *you set yourself up for a long, hard journey.*

The second major weakness in the systematic model of achievement is HOW we go about achieving our goal. Again, our culture is a major influencer. You may have been taught that you need to be strategic—think, plan, act, evaluate, and do it all over again. If you do this long enough, you eventually get there. Built into this model are some strong beliefs that achieving a goal takes time, requires hard work, and is somewhat lonely and competitive. I operated from these beliefs when I pursued goals before my awakening.

Here's how that played out for me. Growing up, I was taught that if you want something bad enough you need to go out and get it yourself. No one will give it to you on a silver platter. So, out I went to earn money starting at age 12. I wanted to do things and buy things my parents weren't able or willing to provide. I worked solo as a baby sitter and office cleaner before getting my first job in a hospital with a group of gals in the dietary department. I took 100% responsibility for my success. However, for a long time, I also believed that taking 100% responsibility meant I had to take 100% of the actions; no one was going to help me to accomplish my goals. Over time, I learned otherwise; but for many of my goals, I suffered in silence, believing it was all on me to achieve. I hated asking for help. I thought I would be judged as weak or lazy for asking. Does that resonate with you? The harder I worked, the prouder I was of my efforts. I took pride in telling my parents, friends, or partner how hard I was working.

I now see how limiting this approach is. How much can we truly accomplish if we have to go it alone? As bigger and bigger callings bubble up, I've come to experience firsthand how the narrow focus of *have to/need to/should do it all myself* limits my impact. Saying *yes* to my bigger callings has pushed me to seek assistance to bring my projects to life. While this initially was very hard for me to do—I needed to give up control as well as more clearly articulate my vision to others—these projects have been my most rewarding.

Because the model of systematic achievement is more fixed on being structured, strategic, and working hard, it is severely limited! It requires us to spend time in our head, connecting with our brain/our intellect and disconnecting with our body and inner wisdom. Have you ever felt you were living your life from the neck up (i.e., all in your head)? I did for many years.

We are growing more conscious individually and collectively and learning that achievement alone does not bring happiness or fulfillment. How many people have you seen that "have it all," but have nothing that's really important to them? They have the house, the car, the vacations, but they have sacrificed everything to achieve it. They've lost their relationships, damaged their health, and totally forgotten themselves and their true essence in the world. I had a taste of this before my personal awakenings. Thank goodness for my awakenings that shocked me back into feeling and connecting with my authentic self again! You surely have found ways to achieve your goals, but has success come with a personal price that blocks your full potential, fulfillment, and Radiance?

***Women face an epidemic of overwork, over-efforting;
this calls for a soul-centered model of achievement.***

Women everywhere struggle with overwork, exhaustion, and lack of fulfillment. Feelings of depression and isolation are common. Women have bought into cultural conditioning around achievement that makes them push for results rather than connect with their core Radiance to realize their greatest callings and dreams. Many women have come to believe that to achieve something significant, they have to give their livelihood. Driving and pushing from this do-or-die mindset leaves women stressed-out and unfulfilled.

Not a pretty picture, right? This epidemic stems from believing and internalizing a model for achievement that disconnects us from our essence and intuition. Instead, we put trust and faith in information, people, and systems external to ourselves. While women accomplish amazing things in every aspect of life, *so, so, so* many women do it at the high cost of their personal happiness and fulfillment. We need to retire this model *of success at all costs.* It's time for a new paradigm around achievement.

The world will keep on spinning and a new day will dawn every 24 hours. The overall pace of life is getting faster, but we can make a conscious decision to set and pursue our goals in an entirely different way. It requires courage and trust to decide to live differently, to be someone different, and to pursue and achieve from a more conscious and holistic perspective. I invite you to continue the Radiant Achievement journey with me into the next chapter. Discover what this new approach to achievement is all about. It is well worth the journey!

***A Pause for Reflection: Understanding Your
Relationship with Systematic Achievement***

In this reflection, you have the opportunity to pause and review your own experience and relationship to Achievement and the model you currently use. Grab your journal or a piece of paper. Find a quiet place to sit and listen without interruption. Take a couple of deep breaths to center yourself and to connect with your inner wisdom. When you are ready, write your responses to these questions:

1. *List your biggest accomplishments in life so far. Write an "I" next to it if it was an inner inspired goal. Write an "E" if it was an external goal as described in this chapter. How many of your key goals were inwardly inspired? How many were external? What pattern do you see?*

2. *What is your relationship with Achievement?*

   Consider how you feel in your day-to-day life. Are you depleted, stressed out, stuck, or unfulfilled? How does this affect your relationship with Achievement? Consider if you are you living life on the edge of burnout as you continue to push, push, push toward your goals. Have you achieved success, but feel empty on the inside? Write down what comes up for you.

3. *What is your personal definition of Achievement up to now?*

4. *What has your experience been with systematic achievement as described in this chapter, including any obstacles or effects you have experienced?*

5. *In what ways have you been over-efforting, overworking, and overdoing with regard to your goals?*

BONUS MATERIAL

Enter "800004" in the Radiant Achiever APP TRACK NOW page to unlock additional content related to this chapter.

CHAPTER 2

The New Approach is Radiant Achievement

Radiant Achievement is an innovation using inner powers you already possess.

What if you could be energized (rather than burned out) by the pursuit of goals and achievements? What if you found the courage and strength to pursue your deeper desires? What if your approach to achievement enlivened your authentic self and your conscious awareness of what you do and the impact it has? What if that ultimately made you more radiant and turned on to live a fulfilling life? All this and more is possible through an empowered solution that turns traditional achievement on its head.

The solution for the achievement crisis you've experienced up to now is to reframe how you define and approach achievement—specifically, to reframe achievement through seven innate powers that allow for more of your natural essence to inform and inspire your actions and achievement. Using this new paradigm, you will feel more, be more connected to yourself and others, have more joy and ease in your life, and feel turned on about your life and all that you are accomplishing! That's a big promise. Before I dive into the specifics of this new approach, let me share how I came to reconnect with my own path of Radiant Achievement.

RADIANT ACHIEVEMENT

*Two wakeup calls jolted me off my conditioned
path and into a Radiant Awakening.*

Two significant wakeup calls inspired my rediscovery of Radiant Achievement. First, in the spring of 2014, I received an unexpected diagnosis: I had early stage, non-invasive breast cancer. With barely a pause, I jumped into research and strategy mode. In a short time, I put a plan together to heal myself within 18 months (my old strategic thinking in action!). It seemed like the logical thing to do, though I also made some other changes, like taking time to journal, reflect, and slow down.

In the middle of this plan, a mere nine months later, I received my second big change, this one even more painful than the first. After 21 years and one especially painful evening of frank conversation, my marriage came to a crashing HALT. It wrenched my core. There was no going back, no reconciling, things were over. In that dark, lonely moment, my life as I knew it was gone. Although I had subconsciously begged for something to change, I pleaded with God that this WAS NOT what I asked for. The crash of my marriage devastated me. This time my healing required more than just a plan.

I connected with a strong inner calling that told me to LET GO, to let go of my life as I knew it. I could not ignore that message. While it took some months, I ultimately realized that holding on would only hurt me. In one quiet moment, alone by myself, I faced all my old plans, strategies, conversations, thoughts, and hopes about my life, my relationship, and my future. Then, in one fell swoop, I RELEASED it all. Feeling a palpable shift in that moment, I realized that I had also released the energetic and emotional baggage that came with the unfulfilled plans, dreams, and ideas of my old life.

Next, I was inspired to do a deep-dive self-inquiry. I knew that I would need more than just good self-care to get me through this shocking, life-altering situation. Although I had already implemented some healthy habits—journaling, walking on the beach, connecting with positive, uplifting people—I sensed that I needed to look deeply into who I had become and to reconnect with my true essence. It seems I had forgotten about that.

I craved clarity about how I got myself into both the cancer and the divorce. Given the extreme pain of the divorce, I knew in my heart that any forthcoming growth would be nothing compared to the heartbreak I felt at the moment. It has been said that when the student is ready, the teacher will appear. This was exactly what happened to me.

Every journey begins with one step. Mine
began by saying YES to an email.

There I was at the start of my new journey, one I was consciously choosing. I secretly hoped it would take me to new places, new ideas, and an entirely new paradigm for my life and my business. I stumbled onto an email for a free one-hour workshop, and that workshop led to a group program that was the perfect answer for me. I couldn't believe it! How amazing that I just happened to see this email and that it just happened to be EXACTLY what I was looking for! Every fiber of my being jumped for joy. For the next several months, I dove deeply inward. I was amazed to see myself so differently, to see how I had been carrying an identity and a story that affected how I showed up for me, for others, and in the world, and it turned my belief system upside down.

I started to consciously love and appreciate
me, and shifts started to happen.

While I went through the program, another event happened. My bathroom at that time had a white tile countertop with white grout. While I don't wear a lot of makeup, I can be a bit messy. To save myself and my cleaning lady from extra work, one day I plopped an eco-friendly paper towel on the counter before applying my makeup. I dumped my makeup bag onto the paper towel and proceeded to put on my makeup. I looked at my reflection in the mirror for longer than usual. I peered into my eyes and looked deeply at the woman who was me. I recognized her and felt affection for her, but I felt somehow disconnected from her. I offered a quick smile and then finished applying my makeup.

My little paper towel trick was working well. It kept my countertop clean, and I contained my mess—a small beauty victory for me! I was pretty excited (can you tell I'm easily pleased?). I remembered the lingering look at my reflection from the previous day, and when I did this for the second time, I realized something big. I DID NOT FEEL beautiful. I felt, well, kind of flat.

Have you ever looked at someone you love and your heart got all revved up and happy? Well, I didn't feel that way about myself. It hit me that I no longer wanted to feel this way, regardless of what had or hadn't happened to me. I intuitively knew that the image I saw and the feeling I felt didn't reflect the "true me." Ever so bravely, I said (with a smile on my face), "Hello, beautiful." I didn't go crazy and say it with any degree of overenthusiasm; I simply said in a warm and honest way. "Hello beautiful." Hmmmmm, that felt pretty good. Let me say it again. "Hello beautiful." This time I added a little smile at the end, and "ting," I felt something in my heart. I think my heart liked what I had to say. I committed to do this mirror work again the next day.

I continued this morning process for a week or so, laying out a fresh paper towel, doing my makeup, looking in the mirror and saying like a mantra, "Hello beautiful." At the end of the first week, I was feeling guilty about throwing the paper towel away every day. As a minor adjustment to my morning beauty ritual, I decided to save the paper towel. It may not sound significant but having this paper reminder each morning reminded me to do my uplifting mirror work. I threw the used paper towel away at the end of the week. Besides the shift to use the towel for a week, I was making another shift. I was shifting how I felt about me! After just a couple of weeks, I truly began to feel beautiful. Could my simple, daily ritual of mirror work really have this much impact?

My inner shifts reconnected me to my creativity—
that place where my Radiance resides.

Back in those days, I was journaling EVERYTHING about my life. I captured the sad, tearful moments, the new insights I gained in my coursework, and my paper towel and mirror work activities. Capturing these new creative moments in detail in my journal was uplifting. It was like watching the first buds of spring break through the soil, just warming up from winter. They were signs of hope and possibility for something beautiful to emerge.

As the days warmed up, so did my creativity. I inquired within myself, "Instead of throwing the paper towel away every week, what if this makeup mat was fabric that could be washed?" I answered myself, "Good idea!" (Can you relate to these internal conversations?) "And, what if you had different affirmations or mantras on different themes?" Again, I answered myself, "Good idea." I made several phone calls to my good friend Holly. I had to share this with someone outside my swirling brain. She gave me a thumbs up each time we spoke and encouraged me to stick with my ideas. After the third time I called her, she said we need to meet, and I agreed.

As I gathered my things for our meeting, I sensed that something big was stirring in me. I felt like I had when I first announced to friends that I was pregnant—nervous excitement from knowing something beautiful has started but not being sure about the journey ahead. It felt bigger than just my product idea. I knew that whatever unfolded, I was in good hands with my friend.

I arrived at the coffee shop filled with anticipation about what she would say when I shared more details of my vision. I felt equal shares of excitement and trepidation. The CALLING I felt in my body was palpable. I brought out the paper towel sample I had drawn up; I shared my vision for the designs and the fabric; I said that I wanted it to be created locally and in a sustainable way. I was more and more energized with each word I spoke, until it hit me: This was NOT only about bringing a product to life. It was about me reclaiming my desire to live my fullest, most authentic, fulfilling, purposeful, turned-on life!

On that one average day, sitting in a coffee shop with my dear friend, I was inspired to make a bold and dramatic commitment, one that would forever alter my life's trajectory. I drew a line in the sand and proclaimed: *From this day forward, I will ACHIEVE, LEAD, and LIVE my life by honoring and following the callings of my soul, no matter how small or how big they feel.* I knew in my body that I would never abandon myself again.

I realized that these deep, innate callings were in my DNA. They were part of my uniqueness and my life's purpose. These callings, I realized, were the seeds of MY true Radiance! That ordinary day became extraordinary. In making my declaration, my whole body shivered. I took a stand for my innate worth, something from which I had been disconnected. My radiant awakening, to reconnect with and take a stand for my worth, opened my heart to fully and wholeheartedly love me for who I am.

I cried, I laughed and then I said *yes*. I needed no permission for this *yes*. I had no need to feel bad or apologize for what I wanted. I was saying *yes* to all of me, and I was also saying *yes* to bringing this product to life. I flashed back to years past and other product ideas I had, but never followed through on. A loving sadness bubbled up in me. I paused to remember these old ideas, I sent a heartfelt blessing to each of them, and then I forever let them go from my thoughts. I shifted my attention back to the present and realized *I am finally doing it—bringing my product idea to life!* I was excited and nervous all at once, partly because I was out of my comfort zone. This went against all my adult conditioning. *Was my idea worthy enough?* Even though the worth question popped up right away, this time I was prepared to look behind the curtain to see what prevented me from fully owning that question.

In committing to be okay not having my path all figured out, I ignited my new path of Radiant Achievement.

15

Another part of my excitement and nervousness came from my monumental commitment to be okay, even though I hadn't figured it all out. Given my long history of planning, this would be a big change for me. Further, I committed to be open to accept help and guidance from wherever it came. I wanted my life to flow with grace and ease. I knew the days of pushing and over-efforting to make things happen were behind me. This milestone actually triggered something else—it awakened me to the next phase of my life's work.

I set to work on bringing my makeup mat idea to life, but where exactly should I start? This goal, this project was different. Bringing this dream to life felt exactly like when I decided to compete in fitness-related figure competitions. It was a full-bodied *yes*. I K-N-E-W in my body (felt it in my body) that I was ABSOLUTELY, NO DOUBT, HELL YES, going to bring this idea to life! And for the first time in many years, I knew I didn't have to know how.

I didn't have to know the way. I trusted that I'd find the way (or rather, the way would find me), one step at a time. And that's exactly what happened. Along my twisty, turny, up-and-down, fast-flowing and slow-going journey to bring my Mantra Makeup Mat™ to life, I gradually discovered the Powers of Radiant Achievement. It wasn't until I launched the product that I could look back and clearly see my own wonderful, amazing powers—powers I had had all along. I no longer needed to search frantically or fearfully for the "perfect" external expert to give me guidance. I had all the powers I needed.

How is Radiance connected to achievement?

Oprah Winfrey is famous for *what I know for sure*. Well, what I know for sure is that ***ALL WOMEN are naturally radiant***. It's not something we have to work at—we are born radiant. I am, you are, your mom, girlfriends, sisters, neighbors, and co-workers. I mean EVERY woman. We don't all **show** our Radiance (we'll get to that later), but we are born with it inside us. What was your experience as a little girl? Did you have a vibrancy to your smile? A twinkle in your eyes? A skip in your step? A song that you sang? If so, those were outward signs of your connection to your inner Radiance. As little girls, until something comes along to dull it, our Radiance is pure; our light hasn't been dimmed by false beliefs, limiting stories, or fearful family members. I remember laughing, skipping, and dancing as if no one were watching, and I felt vibrant. Radiant Achievement, the new model of achievement, reignites these qualities and more.

I have shared key definitions for *achievement*. It's important to do the same around R*adiance*. I know that I desire to BE radiant, and I want you to enjoy that benefit too. Merriam-Webster.com defines *radiance* as "marked by or expressive of love, confidence or happiness." And the term *radiant* has two great definitions on Dictionary.com that represent the effects of using the Powers of Radiant Achievement:

1. *emitting rays of light; bright; shining*
2. *bright with joy, hope, etc.*

Throughout this book, I capitalize the word *Radiance,* as it is the overarching theme. Have you ever experienced someone as "expressive of love, confidence or happiness"? Have you ever felt so full of joy or hope that you felt bright and you emanated a shining glow about you? That is Radiance!

I believe we have an inner AND outer Radiance. To the degree that we connect with and honor our inner Radiance, we see it reflected as outer Radiance. What exactly do I mean by *inner Radiance*? This was one of my favorite discoveries during my transformational journey. Our inner Radiance is connected to the quiet rumblings of our passions and desires. Said another way, these inner rumblings are the seeds of our Radiance. Many times, our quiet rumblings are connected to our natural gifts and talents. My connection to my creativity enabled me to receive the intuitive hits to create my Mantra Makeup Mat™. When I engaged with this rumbling (my desire) and worked to bring it to life, I felt a physical energy and glow that I could see, and so did many friends and other people I met. People actually commented on how vibrant I looked and how powerful I sounded.

When you glow, you emit a magnetic energy that draws people and opportunities to you. I saw this firsthand as I created and launched my product. On multiple occasions, I shared my product with someone and they gave me the name of a shop owner or a website or a lead for a speaking engagement. This magnetism drew things to me without effort on my part to make it happen.

For your Radiance to shine its brightest, for you to live your most authentic, fulfilling life, you need to tap into both parts of the Radiance equation. Here is where achievement comes into play. On the one side, connect with your inner desires. As I explained above, these are the seeds of your inner Radiance. Then germinate these seeds by creating (achieving or expressing) something into the world—your goal or intention. These callings can't be pursued with the old systematic model of achievement if you want them to reach their full potential. These goals invite you to approach achievement in a new, more empowering, creative, joyful, intuitive way—the way of **Radiant Achievement**.

Radiant Achievement is a new way to innovate achievement that is inspired by your soul, nurtured through your creativity, and acted upon by your intuitive energy.

Radiant Achievement, simply stated, is the manifestation of a goal, dream, or desire that was first created from an inner calling or desire and then brought to life by connecting with and engaging core powers you innately possess. Let me restate this: You ALREADY possess these powers. I affectionately refer to these powers as the **Powers of Radiant Achievement**. These powers allow you to connect with and bring to life (manifest) your own expression of Radiance.

Radiant Achievement and the powers that are part of this approach to achievement reconnect you to your inner, authentic essence, to your soul. This is not fluff—it is powerful connection to your full range of innate energetic qualities. These are not qualities you need to learn; they are part of you, waiting to be activated and embodied. Classified into two main themes, you have *allowing* qualities and *performing* qualities to tap into. The allowing qualities let things come to you with ease and grace. Allowing qualities include intuition, creativity, receptivity, and patience. Performance qualities are your link to execution. Performance qualities include action, logic, reason, and control. One set of qualities is not more important or better than the other. Both are necessary. In this approach to achievement, they all work synergistically together. It is the perfect blend of opposites that you engage intuitively, as you will learn in the coming chapters.

By engaging these powers, you can more deeply connect with your personal callings and desires; you understand more fully that your purpose is bigger than yourself; following these callings is the path to fulfill your purpose; and the path itself empowers you and brings out your authentic self. The Powers of Radiant Achievement are the magic to intuitively pursue your goal with grace, ease, and deep trust. These powers open you to curiosity and wonder. These powers evoke so much self-love that you cannot NOT pursue your inner callings.

Radiant Achievement is a beautiful use of both sets of innate energies in a balanced and fluid way that not only gets you to your goal, but allows you to grow, expand, and shine along the way. Does this sound like a terrific way to pursue your goals?

If you haven't yet bought into this new way, think about how you've been achieving your goals and dreams up to now—if, in fact, you are doing so. Have you ever forced yourself to do something even if you lacked energetic connection to the task? Even though it didn't resonate with you as valid, you did it because you felt you "should"? Or you constantly second guessed your decisions and next steps? Or you felt stalled from movement until you could poll your friends or partner to see what THEY thought you should do? Or you desire something in your life, but it's just not happening?

Maybe you are at the other end of the spectrum—a high achiever who succeeds often but is never truly satisfied. Are you in a cycle of barging ahead to pursue the next goal without acknowledging or appreciating your previous success? Over time, I have done all of these things. But all that doubt and frustration and urgency melted away when I implemented the core Powers of Radiant Achievement. The same can happen for you!

Understanding and using the Powers of Radiant Achievement is different from any other program or process I have learned about achievement. Radiant Achievement isn't a model at all. Here are some key things to know about the powers and new way of achieving:

1. **They require some learning or relearning.**

   While the Powers of Radiant Achievement are innate, you need conscious learning to reconnect with and engage them. Past conditioning from family and environment may have disconnected you from some or all of these powers. You still have them, but now they lie dormant. Awakening them is like rebuilding a muscle that has atrophied.

2. **These powers are not yet another process that you need to learn.**

   A fabulous thing about Radiant Achievement and use of your powers is that the process is fluid—as you tap into your powers, the next logical steps naturally unfold. I recommend that you consciously commit to embody these powers more and more each week, so that it becomes habit.

3. **There is no start or stop point.**

   It does not matter which power you engage first. You can engage in more than one power at the same time. As you learn the powers and apply them, you will feel into where to focus first. That means you will connect with your body and your intuition to hear where to start. If this sounds foreign or scary at first, that's okay. I'll teach you how to feel it into your body. The bottom line is that there is no right or wrong place to start implementing your powers.

4. **Use of your Powers of Radiant Achievement creates a ripple effect.**

As you engage your powers, your fullest possibilities slowly ignite and become evident. I have experienced this in myself and have seen it to be true for other women, too. When I first pursued my makeup mat project, I saw only the product, the beautiful fabric mat. As I stepped forward and connected with a deeper message to make this something to support women in transforming the love, appreciation, and belief in themselves, that led me to create the Mindful Moment Radiance Ritual that is now part of the package.

Here's one way the ripple effect showed up for me. Once I launched the product including the Radiance ritual, I felt called to teach women how to perform the ritual. I spoke to some small audiences, which sparked a vision and desire to speak my message to larger audiences. I wrote in my journal about this and many other examples and was delighted to watch the synchronistic unfolding of my life and purpose. It all came from saying *yes* and to letting things unfold without trying to control every aspect.

I gained an insight from Dr. Barbara DeAngelis' book *Soul Shifts* that I read during my healing period. The book spoke about how to connect more deeply with our soul and to listen to it. I learned that our soul will slowly reveal our purpose. It doesn't happen all at once, but in increments that we can easily handle. As we take small steps forward and achieve what calls to us, a bigger purpose is then revealed. We don't need to judge how small or how big our calling is. We simply need to pursue it. That is the beauty of Radiant Achievement. When you activate the Powers of Radiant Achievement, you step not only toward your soul calling, but toward discovering and fulfilling your purpose.

5. **Radiant Achievement is the new foundation for Radiant Leadership.**

Do you resonate with being a leader, or is your gut reaction, *I'm not a leader*? If you don't see yourself at the very least as the leader of your life, then you may be missing out on reaching your fullest potential and fulfillment. I say this with love and compassion, because I stood silently for numerous years hoping someone would tap me and say, "You are the leader of your life." We are all leaders in some way.

I had to learn that no one would give me the permission to lead either my life or my own company. If you haven't already done so, stand up and vote for yourself as a leader. When you lead with your Powers of Radiant Achievement, you expand your Radiance!

In the next section of this book you will learn about your innate powers—the Powers of Radiant Achievement:

1. The Power of Authentic Self Worth
2. The Power of Mindset
3. The Power of Inner Listening
4. The Power of Inspired Action
5. The Power of Commitment

6. The Power of Reflection
7. The Power of Ritual

Are you ready to awaken your vibrant Radiance? Are you ready to lay down your old methods of systematic achievement and consciously give rise to Radiant Achievement? All that is required is to decide that now is the time. NOW is the time for every woman to listen to the callings of her soul, engage her gifts and talents, and manifest her callings in the world. Women need this. The world needs this.

Decide now, before you read on. Examine your life and the goals you are working on or the goals and dreams you want to work on but have not yet started. Write notes about the ideas that come to you. Let's *activate* your Radiant Achievement. If you want a deeper dive than is offered in this book, see the Company Contact Information section for ways to work with me or participate in one of my core programs.

*A Pause for Reflection: Understanding Your Relationship
with Your Radiance and Radiant Achievement:*

*In this reflection, you will pause to examine your own experience and relationship
to your radiance and your Radiant Achievement. Grab your journal. Find a
quiet place to sit and listen without interruption. Take a couple of deep breaths
to center yourself and to connect with your inner wisdom. When you are ready,
write your responses to the following questions:*

1. *How connected am I with my Radiance?*

2. *When have I felt or been the most Radiant? What was I doing,
   saying, or being?*

3. *As I review my list of key accomplishments from the previous
   chapter, are there other goals to add to the list that come from my
   inner callings and desires? How are these goals different from other
   external goals I have pursued?*

4. *When I look at the list of the Powers of Radiant Achievement, which
   ones am I most interested to explore more? Which ones bring up
   resistance? Why?*

5. *What about the new model of achievement excites me? What
   scares me?*

6. *Where in my life am I currently leading?*

7. *Where do I have the ability to lead, but have shied away from taking
   the lead?*

BONUS MATERIAL

*Enter "800005" in the Radiant Achiever APP TRACK NOW page to unlock
additional content related to this chapter.*

PART 2

Activating the Powers of Radiant Achievement

These innate powers, when activated and embodied, awaken your highest potentials for a radiantly fulfilling and turned-on life.

CHAPTER 3

The Power of Authentic Self-Worth

***The Power of Authentic Self-Worth is about
confidence, self-love, and owning who YOU are.***

Self-Worth is a hot topic in our world. We are engulfed by comparison, products, and media messaging that tells us we are not okay as we are. It's out of control. Let's steer the self-worth ship back in a positive direction. We will do it when we each accept our part—owning our worth.

Authentic Self-Worth is knowing you are enough always and in all ways. Say that several times out loud. "I AM ENOUGH ALWAYS. I AM ENOUGH IN ALL WAYS." You lack nothing. You are worthy just as you are. You have nothing to prove. Authentic Self-Worth has nothing to do with perfection, my dear friend. You were born worthy, and self-worth resides deep in your heart and soul.

When you connect with and own your Authentic Self-Worth, you love and appreciate who you are, as you are. You know that you are whole and complete. You feel confident. You know that you don't need fixing. While there are ways you want to change (from a loving perspective of growth and expansion), you know you are not broken. Connected with Authentic Self-Worth, you see the value of your ideas, desires, and callings. You own your desires without feeling bad or having to explain or justify it. That was my struggle with my self-worth.

For many years as a married woman, I doubted my ideas, saw them as trivial and unimportant. Frequently giving up on my idea, I would defer to my then husband's or children's desires. I did this about family weekend outings, about how to raise our children, and even about dates I wanted to have with my husband. Pushback from anyone about an idea of mine made me give in to keep the peace. I was unable to stand up for my vision of a family unit. I essentially treated myself as a second-class citizen. I spent a lot of time explaining what I wanted and why, as if I had to apologize for being me. While my heart ached in these moments, it took years to see the full impact on me. I denied myself time and time again, showing myself that I wasn't important.

A strong connection to your Authentic Self-Worth
is required for your most fulfilling life.

Authentic Self-Worth is a cornerstone for a fulfilling and radiant life. Without it, we can live a good life, and we may even achieve some of our deeper goals, but we will not be our most expressed and radiant self. Without Authentic Self-Worth, we feel undeserving of what we have, that we don't measure up, or that it is selfish to pursue what we desire. How limiting this is! A multitude of teachers today speak of the importance of self-worth. They have studied, researched, trained, and written books on the many aspects of self-worth. While I don't claim to be an expert, I know from my experience that the instant I started owning my worthiness for who I was in that present moment my life dramatically changed. Internally, I felt a power rise up in me that I hadn't felt since I was in my early twenties, a power that said I am awesome. With this inner power, my belief in myself was palpable. Externally, I began to do things I had not allowed myself to do in the past. I took dance lessons. I started saying *no* without a long-winded explanation. And perhaps the biggest shift in owning my worth is that I found the courage to pursue what called to me, no matter how big or small. I refer to these as my soul-centered callings.

A soul-centered calling might sound scary for someone who has been focused on external goals with a model of systematic achievement, disconnected from her inner voice. While it feels scary to say *yes* to these innate callings, that is where fulfillment lies. Soul-callings come in all sizes and shapes. The common thread is that your inner voice or higher self is calling you to them. They are sourced from inside. Your soul calling might feel and sound like that thing you feel you were put on this earth to do. It might feel that big. Or it might be smaller, something that you feel energized about without knowing why. You simply sense that it's in your highest interest to say *yes* and that it will lead to bigger things.

Either way, you are born with these callings deep, deep, inside you. You don't decide your calling; it has already chosen you. If you are thinking that you have no idea what your calling is, that you have never experienced this, I offer an exercise in Chapter 5 on the Power of Inner Listening that can support your discovery of your current callings.

When I owned my worth, I opened myself to hear and pursue my current soul-calling: *to inspire, teach, and guide women to be their most radiant and fulfilled selves by pursuing their soul-calling using the Powers of Radiant Achievement!* This is why Authentic Self-Worth is one of the Powers of Radiant Achievement.

While we are born with self-worth, it can
be blurred and clouded over time.

In my younger days, I had a strong sense of self-worth. I was confident, vocal about my ideas, and courageous to pursue my dreams. I felt that I had a secret no one knew. That secret was a strong feeling that I was special. Indeed, I was special, and I have come to realize we are all special in our own way. That was my Authentic Self-Worth in action.

On my path of being a corporate woman turned stay-at-home mom living a fast-paced life, wanting to please my type-A-personality husband, and "have it all," I slowly forgot that I was special. I began to see myself as a helper and supporter for others and believed their needs and preferences were more worthy than my own. I remember painful moments when I was afraid to speak up for what was in my heart, thinking it was selfish to have these yearnings. On top of that, I heard an old conditioned message—my ideas were crazy. How disempowering is that?

Self-worth is never an either/or.

While I had made a commitment to first support my family, I had also adopted a belief that it was an either/or, that I had to choose between caring for myself or caring for my family. Over the years, this took a heavy toll on me, my worth, and my Radiance. Three things happened: (1) I began to disconnect from my feelings. I pushed away feelings of unfulfillment and pain for not pursuing what mattered to me. (2) Disconnection from my feelings caused me to live more in my head. (3) Living in my head created stress and anxiety, further removing me from my worth and Radiance.

Year after year of giving up and giving in on my own desires, I created a new pattern. A pattern of strategy, planning, and problem solving kept me busy and clouded the fact that I was not owning my worth and loving myself. If I really wanted something, I created a strategy and plan to get it without it appearing that "I just wanted it." I believed I needed to justify what I wanted and that a plan would do that. I also believed that if I had a really good plan, I'd be less likely to get pushback from my then-husband. Oh, the pain I put myself through to protect my true feelings from being rejected! I was no longer that vibrant, fun-loving woman with an easy, outgoing personality.

Deep callings did pop up periodically, such as my desire to compete in fitness-related figure competitions. The last time this occurred was in 2012, right after I turned fifty. Initially, it felt selfish to say I wanted to pursue this goal. I already felt overwhelmed as a corporate wife, mother of two active teenagers, and part-time entrepreneur. On the one hand, the calling was so deep, so authentic, that I knew I had to do it for my soul's sake. On the other hand, I was worried about pushback from my family that it would affect my availability to support them. They would need to help and support me, and it took every fiber of my being to stand up and say I wanted to compete again. I am so grateful that I did! Taking a stand for myself provided a glimmer of hope for joy and fulfillment in my life that had felt overwhelming and out of control for so long.

So, some 28 weeks later, I competed. I took two first-place trophies and one overall trophy! It was a moment I will never forget. My body overflowed with joy, love, and gratitude for what I had done and for ME! My high lasted several weeks after the competition. I woke up every morning ready for a new day, confident I could handle anything that came my way. Feeling proud of myself for honoring my desire, I experienced spontaneous moments of deep gratitude for my commitment to bring my goal to life. I had finally reconnected with my true self. This was the beginning of a new chapter in my life. Or so I thought.

Something unexpected happened. Little by little, I returned to my old way of being, the beliefs, thoughts, and actions of my well-practiced roles of supportive wife, mother, and part-time entrepreneur. As life eventually returned to its old speed and routine, something felt different, heavier. I didn't realize it at the time, but my choice of figure competition and taking care of me had been a saving grace. It awakened a subconscious part of me that I had been denying, numbing, and quieting for years.

You may have heard that sometimes things need to get worse before they get better. That was the case for me. Not only was I back to my old self and denying my own needs, but everyone else seemed to be having issues. I felt more and more disconnect with my husband, and we disagreed on a regular basis. My daughter was on an emotional roller coaster regarding her studies, and my son was dealing with his own version of teen troubles. I longed for things to change, to have peace in the house and for the pace of life to slow down. Especially, I longed to be that awakened, joyful, empowered and alive woman once again. My inner request was soon granted through two wakeup calls.

My healing journey helped me reconnect with and reclaim my self-worth.

My wakeup calls, like all wakeup calls, were rich with learning and growth. They started with core lessons about self-worth. I could probably write an entire book about my journey of seeing and owning my worth. As I write these words to you now, I feel so much love and appreciation for me. My acknowledgment of that expands my heart-energy, and I feel a warm glow. It is indescribably delicious! So, how did I get to the place of loving myself and owning my worth?

Let me summarize it by saying S-L-O-W-L-Y.

At the time of my divorce, when my heart broke wide open and spilled all over my living room floor, all I could do was cry and journal. Those were acts of love and compassion toward myself, but I don't think I really L-O-V-E-D me at that time. As a commitment to mending my broken heart, I surrounded myself with what made my heart happy. I prayed, I spent time in nature, I had deep conversations with close girlfriends, and I read inspiring books. I felt the healing begin. I began to feel a sense of safety and peace.

As my strength and stability grew, I consciously did something else—I brought wonder and play into my life. I signed up for ballroom dance lessons, which felt awkward at first, but quickly became therapeutic. I felt joy in the upbeat Latin rhythm and moving my body to the beat. Dancing helped me get out of my head and reconnect with my body's inner wisdom. The more I played, the less serious I felt. Life was less heavy. I was optimistic that I could handle whatever came my way, even the divorce mediation in process.

With this newfound confidence and connection to my body's inner wisdom, I took yet another step toward owning my worth. I let myself be curious about my life. I began, consciously at first, to see my life with a sense of childlike inquiry. "I wonder (fill in the blank)" became a daily exercise for me. *I wonder what new life I can create for myself? I wonder how my product idea can come to life? I wonder how I can use my lessons and learnings to positively impact other's lives?* I approached the creation of my makeup mat with a sense of wonder. In my morning affirmation mirror work, I was openly curios. These activities not only brought me joy again, they stoked and nurtured my creativity. And you know what? I started to feel a growing confidence and love for myself.

Then one day, something truly transformational happened. I was working on a talk that would become part of my coaching business. In the middle of writing "my story" (sharing my journey of life of when I was at my lowest point and then how I came out of it to where I was now), and it hit me. I felt (not thought) a big AHA: *I had not felt my worth or authentic love for myself for the last ten years!* **I had not FELT that love!** In that moment of realization, my entire body vibrated. It felt like I was a metal bell being rung at high noon. DDDDDDIIIIIIIIINNNNGGGG! I felt my entire body activated deep into my soul, and simultaneously I felt a rush of love and worthiness for me. I sat for several minutes soaking in this realization and all the deep emotions I felt. I will never forget that moment.

After catching my breath, I realized that I could not expect someone else to love me if I didn't love myself. I saw in my mind's eye that all of my issues and problems had been created by me. I realized that I set the example for others and that I consistently kicked myself to the curb. This learning jolted me to an entirely new lane in life's freeway. I took a stand that day to always love me. I knew that to live a fulfilling, radiant, and turned-on life (which I deeply desired), owning my own worth and loving myself were *critical*!

I drew the line in the sand to own my worth and love myself, and during my mirror work of speaking positive affirmations, one immediate change came. The day after my big aha, I got up as usual, said a brief gratitude for another day of life, had my first cup of coffee, and proceeded to the bathroom to do my ritual. *You are enough. You are okay exactly as you are right now.* Now these statements had an even deeper meaning for me. Every fiber of my body came alive as I looked deep into my eyes and spoke the words out loud. I didn't simply say the words. I viscerally felt that I am enough, that I am okay exactly as I am. Voicing those statements and feeling them in my body not only expanded my sense of worth, it made such a powerful impact that I included them in one of my Mantra Mindset Moments mat designs.

Activating your Authentic Self-Worth begins with gratitude.

In my journey to seeing, connecting with, and owning my worth, I employed different practices. It is important to understand that there are **unlimited** ways to build these powers within you. And the good news is that there is no one right way. I will share several tools that I discovered, but others will occur to uniquely help you build your muscle of self-worth. That is the amazing thing about Radiant Achievement: *When you connect with and use the powers, you will receive the answers you need, not only to achieve your goal but also to further strengthen your own powers.* Here's how to strengthen your self-worth:

1. **First, write a daily list of at least five things you are grateful for about you**. Write it from a place of deep self-observation. Your goal is for deep self-connection, so this is NOT to be a fast, mental exercise. Take a couple of deep breaths, slow down, scan your day, and ask, "How did I show up today that made me proud? What did I do today that made me proud? What thoughts, actions or words can

I acknowledge myself for? What progress did I make today toward loving me?" These are sample questions to prompt your deeper reflection about the beautiful part of you that you can see and acknowledge. Do this with presence and mindfulness, and your daily brilliance in action will become evident.

2. **Do mirror work.** Mirror work connects you with your Authentic Self-Worth, and it's easy to do because it's linked to something you already do. Whether you are the gal who does full makeup each morning or you go for the more natural look and simply brush your teeth and put on a moisturizer, either way, you are already looking in the mirror. No time is easier than first thing in the morning to spend a few minutes loving and appreciating you. My mirror work started when I did my makeup routine. Because I was already looking in the mirror, it was a perfect reminder to connect with and appreciate who I am at my essence. My initial days of mirror work were uncomfortable, especially the first time I said, "I love you" out loud to me. Strange! I did my best to say it with feeling and to let the words land on my body, to actually feel them soak into my body. Over time I approached the mirror as if I were looking at my best friend. Indeed, I was. This helped me to expand my feeling of love for myself. Over time, my mirror work ritual expanded into five simple steps. You can do them too:
   a) Walk to the mirror and look yourself in the eyes.
   b) Take three deep breaths to center yourself.
   c) Greet yourself with a hello and your name.
   d) Say three things you love and appreciate about you.
   e) Recite your favorite mantra.

Perform each step with mindful presence and feeling. It will create a visceral experience where you focus on feeling love, appreciation, and gratitude for yourself, where you consciously greet yourself. Find an instructional video of my own five-step process in my Radiant Achiever app under the topic *EMPOWERMENT.*

3. **Change your story about your worth.** Sometimes we aren't even aware that we carry stories about unworthiness. We simply think, "This is who I am." I am here to say that if you believe yourself to be anything other than divine, you likely are telling yourself false stories. The good news is that you don't need to have a crisis to change your beliefs. I am going to share some simple ways to become conscious of your stories and one method I used repeatedly when I was in the middle of my transformation. I still use it today when old stories pop up.

   a) Adopt the belief that life is talking to you at all times and that information is all around you to reveal your beliefs.

   b) Make a conscious commitment to be open and curious about how you show up day to day. Observe where you thrive and where you struggle.

   c) In the areas where you struggle, what thoughts and beliefs do you hold? Be conscious of your self-talk. Listen for repetitive messages and thoughts that come up daily. Are you critical and judgmental of others? Are you critical and judgmental of yourself? Do you beat yourself up for what you do, for what you don't do, for your mistakes? Do you resist receiving from others because you feel guilty or unworthy? Write down the messages you hear. Be aware of how often they occur. This is all pertinent information for your transformation!

   d) Armed with information from the previous steps, use this simple process, which I used during my transformation and continue to use today.

i) Pick one of your repetitive beliefs and go into a quiet place to reflect and listen.

ii) Connect to your earliest memory of when you were taught or told you were unworthy. (As an adult, I can see these old situations from an entirely different perspective. While I can see that hurt child, I am no longer that hurt child.)

iii) View the situation objectively from your new perspective, and recognize that whoever told you that story was acting from their own fears and limiting beliefs.

iv) Now look for the deeper truth. The deeper truth is that you are worthy. What can you now see about that old situation that you could not see when you were younger? Choose right now to LET GO of the old story and to consciously write a new story of your worth. (See the bonus section at the end of the chapter for access to additional material for this exercise.)

These stories may be deeply rooted, and your ego will hang onto them until you take enough conscious action to let them go. Depending on how strong a belief is, you may want to use this technique daily as you bring to light different layers of the story that you have piled on to squelch your natural, radiant self over the years. Know that it absolutely is possible to shed your old story of unworthiness and adopt an empowered belief that you are worthy. The one requirement is your willingness and desire to let the old belief go. This can be difficult at first, but stick with it. Stay committed to being your best self.

It's important to know that you don't need a crisis to uncover your limiting beliefs. You can begin to effect change by simply becoming aware when old habits or stories get triggered. Connect with the trigger or story, and then, without judgment, inquire, "I wonder why I do this," or "I wonder why I react this way?" Pausing to focus and reflect on a situation helps you transmute the old story and let it go in the moment, without any deep inner work.

The status quo can be comfortable, especially if we think life is pretty good. But I am here to tell you, vast emotional freedom and growth occur when you let go of old stories.

*A Pause for Reflection: Understanding Your Embodiment
of the POWER OF AUTHENTIC SELF-WORTH*

In this reflection, you can observe your own experience and embodiment of your Power of Authentic Self-Worth. Grab your journal. Find a quiet place to sit and listen without interruption. Take a couple of deep breaths to get centered and to connect with your inner wisdom. When you are ready, write your responses to the following questions:

1. *In what ways am I NOT owning my Authentic Self-Worth?*

2. *In what ways do I see the Power of Authentic Self-Worth in action in my life?*

3. *What next step can I take to more fully embody my Power of Authentic Self-Worth?*

BONUS MATERIAL

Enter "800006" in the Radiant Achiever APP TRACK NOW page to unlock additional content related to this chapter.

CHAPTER 4

The Power of Mindset

***The Power of Mindset includes your conscious
and subconscious thoughts and beliefs.***

Facebook and Instagram are wildly popular platforms for the sharing
of quotes containing positive messages. Meant to uplift, inspire, and
empower the reader to a new Mindset about themselves and their
life, these messages are rampant in my social media news feed. I see
at least five motivational quotes every time I log in! Has social media
caught on to the Power of Mindset?

Curious, I did some basic research into the popularity of the
tags #mindset and #mindfulness in a few of the most-used online
platforms. What I found astounded me. As of the time of writing
this chapter, I found over 13.7 MILLION Instagram posts linked
to the tag #mindset. Searching the tag #mindfulness on Facebook
brought even bigger numbers—25 million hits on the first forty-six
pages! In checking the online giant Amazon, I found over seven
thousand book titles related to Mindset. What this tells me is that
the world is waking up to the Power of Mindset.

The topic of Mindset is enormous. With seven thousand books
written to date, and this book could easily be number 7001. That is
not my intention. In this chapter I will define the Power of Mindset
within the context of Radiant Achievement to help you see how
Mindset effects results and outcomes, and to empower you to more
consciously use the Power of Mindset to pursue and achieve your

soul-centered calling. If you want to go even deeper into the current research on mind and Mindset, see my list of favorite resources at the back of the book.

What is the Power of Mindset? How do we define it in the context of Radiant Achievement and living your most fulfilling and radiant life? Simply stated, your Mindset includes all your thoughts and beliefs. This bears repeating: ALL your thoughts. ALL your beliefs. While our conscious mind can be aware of some aspects of our Mindset, our subconscious mind plays an even bigger role. Many of our beliefs are stored in the subconscious mind, and we may not even be aware that they exist. They are so deep within our subconscious that they seem to be part of who we are. I'll go into this in more detail, but let me say here: YOU are not your beliefs.

Your Mindset affects how you look at yourself, at others, and at the world.

My early awareness of my Mindset was shortly after college. Having moved from Wisconsin to Arizona, I was in an exciting, but unfamiliar place. I had successfully broken out on my own. I had a new home, new job, and new friends that were now part of my reality. I created this! In my last year of college, I had absolutely no doubt that I would move. My desire was strong, and so was my Mindset. I was fearless. I can honestly say I didn't see any obstacles to hold me back. I only saw next steps.

In these early days as a young adult in an unfamiliar town, I became interested in self-improvement. One of the first personal growth books I ever read was Norman Vincent Peale's *You Can If You Think You Can*. It taught me the power of my thoughts (i.e., Mindset). That book was foundational for my early understanding and belief in my Mindset to create my reality. Over time, I lost connection with that power. I went from being a young woman who had no fear and could accomplish anything she set her mind to, to being a woman, wife, and mother wracked with fears. Unbeknownst

CHRISTINE HOWARD

to me, my fears affected not only the results in my goals, but also the amount of joy and love I experienced (or not). I have come to have a whole new connection and appreciation for my Mindset. I no longer take it for granted, and I see how far reaching its impact is in my life. My biggest realization from my recent inner work is how widespread the impact of Mindset is in everyone's life, including my own.

Your Mindset is linked to EVERYTHING in your life—how you look at yourself, how you look at others, and how you look at the world in general. Think of your Mindset as a system of stories. It is a collection of stories about you in relation to your health and wellness, your career, your sexuality, your intelligence, your home, your relationships, your fun, your faith and spirituality, your finances, your success and achievement. I could go on and on, but you get my point. You have thoughts and beliefs about EVERY area of your life, whether you are conscious of them or not.

You have a whole belief system about others, too. You may believe others can't be trusted or that they are not dependable. Maybe you have more positive beliefs, such as *I am supported by others* or *people understand and love me.* You may have strong beliefs about different cultures, people in certain careers, people with money (or without money), and even beliefs about people who have homes or are homeless.

Finally, you have a belief system about the world in general. A common world belief I often hear is *life is hard* or *life is unfair.* Does that resonate with you? Or maybe your core beliefs about the world have a more positive slant like *life is to be enjoyed* or *life is what you make it.* Knowing how wide-reaching your thoughts and beliefs are, do you see how they powerfully impact your life?

**To create or achieve new things, you need
to escape old thought patterns.**

Whether you are aware of it or not, your Mindset drives your life. Your Mindset is in action each day in numerous ways: (1) in the words you speak out loud; (2) through the self-talk that goes on silently in your head; (3) through your actions and reactions; and (4) through who you are being. Your Mindset also shows up in your feelings and emotions. Strong emotions are linked to deep beliefs held consciously or subconsciously.

In reality, most people are not aware of their thoughts and beliefs, because they have held them all their life. We accept something as true because it's long been a part of our identity. Most (if not all) of our beliefs were formed in our younger years. Parents, grandparents, siblings, teachers, and authority figures all had an influence on the beliefs we carry today. Year after year of thinking and doing the same things has us attracting the same results over and over. That reinforces and further forges the power of our beliefs. They become our reality.

I recall hearing that the average person has about twelve thousand to sixty thousand thoughts a day, and of those, 80% are negative, and 95% exactly repeat thoughts from the day before. If true, that's staggering, don't you think? If this is true, what impact does it have on your ability to successfully pursue your dreams and inner callings? What impact does it have on your ability to achieve a fulfilling and radiant life?

Our Mindset influences our feelings, which influence our actions, which impact our results. How can we create or achieve new things when we are stuck in the same old thought patterns? If we are not conscious of our beliefs, we continue to reinforce them, because we get the same result repeatedly. It's a self-fulfilling prophecy. Have you experienced this?

To live your most radiant life, you must not only be mindful of your thoughts, you must consciously choose them.

The Power of Mindset is astounding in its potential to support you in a radiant and fulfilling life—a life where you not only pursue, but also achieve your soul-calling, your dreams, your desires, and your goals. I think of the Power of Mindset as like gravity. I don't have to see or understand gravity to know it's affecting my life. I just need to see the end result. The good news, though, is that unlike gravity, we DO have the capability to change our beliefs, even the subconscious ones.

To fully utilize the Power of Mindset, it is critical to take responsibility for your thoughts, beliefs, actions, and results. When you take responsibility, you are saying *yes* to awareness of your current thoughts and beliefs. That is the starting point. If this feels overwhelming (*how can I possibly control tens of thousands of thoughts and beliefs?*), know that you don't have to do it one by one. You can change your thoughts and beliefs without knowing or understanding all of them. In many cases, you simply need to stop buying into them. I will get into that in the practices that follow.

Once you are aware of a belief, you can question whether the belief serves you or not. You are the only one who can say whether or not your belief supports your desire. If it does not support you, you get to choose to let it go and adopt a new belief instead. A spiritual teacher told me something that clearly spoke to me: "There are two paths for you—slow and hard, or fast and easy." In that moment, I realized that my Mindset on some topics had me going slow and hard. I was struggling with life instead of flowing with life. I see that the slow and hard path was created by thoughts and beliefs that did NOT serve me. Once I was aware of them, I lovingly let them go. In what areas of your life do you struggle to achieve? Examine the Mindsets you carry.

A quick way to evaluate your Mindset is to ask if it's rigid or radiant.

Is your Mindset RIGID or RADIANT? Not all Mindsets are created equal. Your Mindset can support a radiant life, or it can support a life of pain, struggle, and stuckness. Seeing the differences between the two makes it easier to identify your Mindset and ponder where it might serve you to change.

Let's look at several key qualities of RIGID Mindsets:

- **Judgmental:** judging yourself, someone else, a thing, a place.
  Example: *I am not that smart.*
- **Limiting:** puts you or someone else in a box, limits your potential.
  Example: *I don't have enough time.*
- **Based on conditioning:** you are the way you are due to parents and society, and there is nothing you can do to change it.
  Example: *It's in my DNA to be unlucky. I've been this way my entire life.*
- **Victim-based:** things happen repeatedly that you can't control.
  Example: *My family always takes advantage of me.*

Now, in contrast, let's look closely at several key qualities of RADIANT Mindsets:

- **Non-judgmental:** observation and reflection of a situation, but not defining the person.
  Example: *I am expanding my knowledge every day.*
- **Expansive:** supports you in living and reaching your highest potential.
  Example: *I have plenty of time to do what's important to me.*
- **Based on choice:** you have the ability to choose your path.
  Example: *I am becoming aware of old, conditioned stories that limit me. I choose to let them go and replace them with beliefs that support the achievement of my highest potential.*
- **Co-creator-based:** things happen because you are co-creating your future.
  Example: *I set and honor my boundaries with everyone I interact with, including my family.*

If you evaluate your current Mindsets, you will quickly see if your overall Mindset lifts you up, keeps you stuck, or worst-case, pulls you down! This work is important in order to live your fullest life.

When I honestly looked at my Mindset, I painfully realized how TRUE my thoughts and beliefs had been.

When you begin to be conscious of your thoughts and beliefs, and especially when you start to notice what is not serving you, it is important not to judge yourself. Inner work is sensitive. Often we avoid looking inward, because doing so causes us to judge ourselves about what we find. Self-judgment is not the intention of this work, although I've certainly done my share.

I always thought of myself as a positive person, but I was shocked and amused when I became conscious of my existing Mindset. During my healing journey from my divorce, and also through the development of my makeup mat, I allowed myself to observe my Mindset, and I allowed myself to question and challenge it.

Nothing was off limits. I questioned my thoughts and beliefs about betrayal, about love, about fun, about work and contribution, about receiving, about wealth, about my business, my relationships with family and friends, and especially my thoughts about myself. The more I observed, questioned, and learned, the more I realized that my Mindset was running my life. My deep desire to live my fullest life and pursue my soul-centered callings was on the line here. I made an internal and external commitment to keep peeling back the layers as they emerged, until I was able to get to my core truth, untainted by self-imposed limits.

One significant Mindset for me had been that *to be an entrepreneur, you must struggle.* I was dutifully observing my self-talk, when one day I noticed my repeated use of the phrase *I'm struggling here* in conversations and in silent thought. After several days of observing this, I had to see what was behind the belief and clear it. I used journaling and biofeedback techniques in my clearing process, and it gave me clarity about the source of that belief. As owner of a butcher shop, my dad said often to me and my siblings that owning a business was hard. It was a struggle, and if you got lucky, you could succeed. He further instilled in me that the way to success was through education and a corporate career. I heard his message and stored it.

Thirty years later, I see that the growth of my business has been a struggle. It's crystal clear now. Understanding that that was my dad's belief and his story, I energetically blessed the old story, let it go, and created a new belief for myself around entrepreneurship. That business ownership comes only with struggle is just one of many beliefs I have identified and let go of. I've practiced this a lot, and I find the clearing and re-scripting process energizing and uplifting. I invite you to take this journey yourself.

Activating and strengthening your Mindset
begins in the present moment.

In each moment of our day we have the opportunity to create and reinforce an empowered Mindset. Our work happens in the present moment, in the NOW. It happens one moment at a time, and that's great, because we only need to focus on this one moment—the PRESENT MOMENT. In this narrow focus is the possibility of transformation.

In the present moment is where I experimented with different processes and practices, similar to my work to strengthen my Authentic Self-Worth. As I mentioned in the previous chapter, there is no one right way to do this. The methods that I recommend below worked well for me and for my clients. The list is not all-encompassing. Feel free to experiment with other modalities as they occur to you. The key to build your Mindset is to make a commitment to do so. Then, be open and curious to explore processes and practices that speak to you.

1. **Change your stories.** As I've said earlier, we tell ourselves stories about ourselves. We may believe we are not enough, that

we are too much, that we are un-loveable, or any number of other false stories. Our stories affect how we see others (selfish, for example) and the world (cruel, unkind, not fair). To live to your fullest potential, to be your most radiant self, you must shed the limiting stories and adopt new, empowering beliefs.

This multi-faceted process begins with your awareness that you have stories. Next, you become hyper-observant of your thoughts. Pay attention to the little phrases you say, either silently to yourself or out loud to others.

Write things in your journal, then get inquisitive. *When did I first hear this story? How old was I? Who told me? What do I know about the person/situation that brought me the story? How might they have gotten the story?* Stay in inquiry. Curiosity is power. Now that you are an adult, what do you see is the deeper truth?

When I practiced this about *being an entrepreneur is a struggle*, I quickly saw it as my dad's story, and not a universal truth.

Once you are clear about the deeper truth, take a few moments to write an affirmation or mantra that represents the NEW story you wish to adopt. Put it in your journal and post it in visible places around your home or office. Say it out loud and with feeling. *Embody* the words. You will become what you say and believe.

2. **Do mirror work as outlined in Chapter 3 on Self-Worth.** Say your affirmations and mantras with feeling.

3. **Up-level the words you use daily.** Consciously use words that empower you versus words that make an excuse. Who do you know who overuses the word *try*? How does that word resonate with you? *Try* is a word that limits us. When we say, "I will try to exercise today," we express an attempt to

exercise versus a commitment to do it. It gives us an out, and that restricts our ability to be our best self and achieve our desires. The words *always* and *never* are also disempowering. "I never get any breaks." "I will never get out of debt." And what I hear SO often, "I never have enough time."

Turn this around. Add words of empowerment, gratitude, thanksgiving, and appreciation to your regular thought and speech patterns. "I am doing my best in this situation." "I am using this opportunity to learn and grow." "I am grateful for this opportunity to…" versus "I'm not sure this will work out." Recommit daily to consciously use words of hope and empowerment, and that is what you will experience in your life. Empowering words fuel your Radiance. Rescript your language and your Radiance will grow.

4. **Read a book or take a class on Mindset or mindfulness.** I have read multiple books that speak to the power of our mind and shifting our Mindset to uplift and empower our thoughts and beliefs. I guarantee you can find a book that resonates with you on this topic. I've included a few of my favorites in the Resource section.

5. **Consciously clear subconscious beliefs.** Have you ever listened to the chatter in your head? How much of it do you buy into? Your chatter gives you a good clue about your Mindset and your subconscious beliefs. Many modalities exist that can support you to clear deep, subconscious beliefs that you may not even be aware of. I personally have used sound biofeedback, music, tapping, and meditation to connect with and clear deep blockages. See the Resource section of this book for a list of such experts. Be open about this! Free resources are abundant. Search online for groups, phone apps, and healers that speak about rewiring your subconscious. Follow the energy of what resonates with you. No one size fits all. Something will be perfect for you.

A Pause for Reflection: Understanding Your
Embodiment of the POWER OF MINDSET

In this reflection, you will look at your own experience and embodiment of your Power of Mindset. Grab your journal. Find a quiet place to sit and listen without interruption. Take a couple of deep breaths to get centered and to connect with your inner wisdom. When you are ready, write your responses to the following questions:

1. *In what ways do I see the Power of Mindset in action in my life?*

2. *In what ways have I been limiting my ability to live a radiant life due to my Mindset?*

3. *What next step can I take to more consciously utilize my Power of Mindset?*

BONUS MATERIAL

Enter "800007" in the Radiant Achiever APP TRACK NOW page to unlock additional content related to this chapter.

CHAPTER 5

The Power of Inner Listening

Many of us have been raised to value thinking over listening.

"Use your head." "Think your way through this." "Be logical." "Don't be so emotional." "Don't be such a dreamer." "Where did you get that crazy idea?" Those were some of the messages I received from my father, grandparents, and teachers as I was growing up. Those messages influenced me to undervalue and disconnect from my Power of Inner Listening.

The Power of Inner Listening, I believe, is untapped for many people. Many of us (especially in the Western cultures) have been taught to be listeners of the THOUGHTS OF OUR MIND and not listeners to our INNER WISDOM. At a young age, we learned how to listen to others—our parents, teachers, elders, and authority figures. I'm not knocking thinking, here. We absolutely need to think with our logical brain, and by the end of this chapter, I hope you will also see the great advantages and results that can come when we also listen to our inner wisdom.

Inner Listening is the power that has had the most profound effect on me. Not only has it impacted my personal life; it has also greatly expanded my ability to create Radiant Achievement. I have noticed the most significant change in three areas: (1) The use of this power has given me a sense of peace I never knew possible; (2) It has given me a divine connection to unlimited possibility for my life; (3) It has allowed me to make progress on my goals, dreams, and soul-centered calling with a grace and ease I could never have achieved with my logical mind. This one power helped me see that I can achieve my deepest desires from a place of trust and receiving versus only through thinking and doing. When I understood the impact of this, it permanently altered the trajectory of my life. It's a big statement to make, and I say it with reverence and gratitude. I know all these things are possible for you, too. Let's dive into the specifics of what the Power of Inner Listening is all about.

The Power of Inner Listening is the ability to discern intuitive messages in whatever form they appear.

What do I mean by the Power of Inner Listening? There is a voice (I propose, many voices) that speaks to us in subtle and not-so-subtle ways. Some people call this inner voice our intuition or higher self. It is our connection to the larger Universe, to God, Source, Divine Intelligence, and to all of life. You may be familiar with the concept that we are spiritual beings in physical form. I wholeheartedly believe that. Our inner voice is our connection to the spiritual realm that we come from. Our inner voice connects us with our soul, and its messages guide us to live our purpose.

More good news: We ALL came into this world with an inner voice. Every one of us has a built-in inner voice. Not only did we come equipped with an inner voice, but that inner voice is always talking to us. We receive an unending supply of information, answers, guidance, wisdom, and support when we connect to and hear its messages by engaging our Power of Inner Listening. Our job is to be ready and open to hear the messages.

One perspective that helps you understand this inner voice and connect more easily with it is to imagine your inner voice as someone you have a relationship with. Whether or not you are aware of it, you do have a relationship with your inner voice. Your inner voice walks around with you all day. It works in the background, behind the scenes of your life. It works in subtle ways, and most people not only have not connected with this voice, they don't even listen for it. Let's get familiar with how our inner voice speaks to us.

Everyone is slightly different when it comes to how their inner voice speaks to them. Some people receive these deep messages as feelings in their body; it's a physical sense of knowing. Other people receive flashes of pictures or images. Another common way people get messages is through words—they either have visions of the words (or numbers) or they hear the message via spoken word.

When you engage the Power of Inner Listening, you will discover the various ways your inner voice communicates with you. I often get strong feelings in my body, or I hear or see words. Feeling the message in the body is common for many people. *I had a gut feeling* is an example of intuition speaking to us. I had a gut feeling that something was seriously off in my marriage six weeks before any evidence appeared. After asking my husband about it and hearing his logical answer with my brain, my gut still was unsettled. Those were the days when I still doubted myself. I am so glad I've learned my lesson here!

Sometimes I experience the Power of Inner Listening through messages that come to me right before I wake up in the morning. In a half-asleep, half-awake state on most mornings, I get a download of thoughts, ideas, guidance, and sometimes things to do. Initially, I wasn't writing them down; I thought for sure I would remember them. That was never the case. Now, I dutifully pick up my pen and write on my blank journal page to record the wisdom without thought or judgment. I continue to be amazed by the simple and sometimes deep messages that arise. Some of these messages have reminded me that I am on the right path or that I need to be courageous or organized. I have even been reminded of a specific important task to do. That has been so helpful! Writing ideas and tasks down is not an issue for me, but I sometimes lose sight of the right timing. I have received messages to email a client about their recent progress, to buy a birthday card for my mom (well in advance of her birthday), and to schedule a vet visit for my dog. Messages

CHRISTINE HOWARD

like this, received from my inner voice, help me understand the importance of timing for key tasks.

The more developed your Power of Inner Listening, the more synchronistic messages you will hear during your day.

The fun thing about the Power of Inner Listening is that you can receive messages at any time of day and from any source. Inner Listening can occur when you are in a focused meditation or committed to quiet listening time, which is how I began my journey with this power. However, as I continued to deepen my grounding and centeredness (required for Inner Listening), I started to get messages at all different times—when I was working, speaking with someone, relaxing, reading an email, listening to a podcast, out in nature, or sleeping. Our higher self is ALWAYS speaking to us, looking to help us out with answers, next steps, and ideas for new opportunities. Sometimes the guidance comes directly from our inner voice, and sometimes it comes from an external source.

Our higher self is connected to all of life, so some of that guidance comes from external sources like podcasts, conversations, books, and emails. These unexpected, synchronistic messages that show up in perfect timing create flow, joy, and ease for us. This is the Power of Inner Listening in action—to support your journey to your goals and dreams with minimal effort.

Engaging the Power of Inner Listening allows you to flow toward your goals with grace and ease.

The Power of Inner Listening connects you to your intuition, your creativity, and your potential to receive information and answers that would never have occurred to you. Using this power profoundly affects HOW you achieve your goal. It opens you up to achieve with grace and ease versus struggle and strife. It's hard to accept that concept if you are used to a life of struggle, but trust

54

me—the Power of Inner Listening is the gateway to a life of grace and ease. Your biggest responsibility is to be open to listen.

Do you feel a connection with your inner voice? If so, what ways have you already experienced receiving messages? Pause now to reflect on this and write your insights in a journal. What is one of the most profound messages you have ever received? You will have the chance to build on it with the practices at the end of this chapter.

See if you can relate to this. In the systematic way of achievement (aka the "old" model), our focus was to think our way to our goal. We focused on external strategies and ideas. If you own your own business, how many different strategies have you seen or heard as *the way* to be successful in your business? It's unlimited. It reminds me of all the methods I learned about over the years in search of the perfect diet. I spent years spinning in circles as I searched for some magical answer. Focus on external strategies as a starting point leads to uncertainty and anxiety. *Did I pick the right strategy? How can I tell if this is the one for me?* Like me, you may find yourself flip-flopping through different strategies. Such struggle and strife!

Now, switch this around. Start by connecting with your intuition, your inner wisdom. Tap into your wise self, who already knows about you, your business, your work preferences, your values, and priorities. Ask open ended questions about your next steps, and listen for answers in alignment with your true essence. Alignment with your essence is the foundation of Radiant Achievement, and Inner Listening makes this possible. As I deepened my skills of listening, my actions toward my goal became more fluid. I inquired, listened, heard, and then acted. My days started to flow. I could feel it in my body. I could feel the flow.

I went from living in my head and feeling disconnected from my higher self, to deep connection to my inner wisdom and feeling peace and alignment.

CHRISTINE HOWARD

When I started using this super power, I felt peace and joy. Sadly, I had ignored this power for years, when I was busy and believed I didn't have time to sit and be quiet. Little did I know that I had it all backward. Not only did I previously believe I didn't have time to be quiet and listen, but to make matters worse, I ignored the intuitive messages that did get through to me. I was afraid my life would unravel if I paid attention to the voice that spoke to me. I feared the unknown. What would I find? How would what I hear affect my life? Would my life break into pieces with what I find out? I feared the worst. Between that and the fast pace I was living, it was easy to justify why I had no time for listening.

I now know that sitting and listening is nothing to be feared. Listening is a tool for growth, positive change, and movement toward our innate goals, dreams, desires, and expression of our highest self. If you are in fear of listening, or if you have not been taking the time to listen, I encourage you to take a new perspective on the power and purpose of listening. Your life does not have to break down in order for you to hear your inner wisdom. In fact, it's quite the opposite. If you take the time to stop and listen NOW, you can lessen the impact of a situation and avoid many problems.

Disconnection with my inner voice is why I lived in my head. At times, I was irrational as I fought to make sense of my swirling thoughts (fears, anxieties, problems). I bounced from one issue to the next—my teenage son who challenging his father and me regarding school, curfews, and extracurricular activities; my husband who was coming home later and later without communicating with me; my daughter who was stressed out about a tough engineering curriculum; and my aging great aunt who was battling cancer for the third time. While I desperately wanted to get off the hamster wheel, I lived in fight-or-flight mode and feared the next hot issue.

Back then, I also didn't believe in myself enough to know I could change things. I practically pleaded with my former husband for our life pace to slow down. His reply was, "This is our life." I didn't have his support to change things, and I felt it would be impossible by myself. One minor refuge was journaling. I paused periodically to dump my thoughts onto paper, releasing the negative stuff onto the empty pages. Journaling relieved enough pressure to keep me going. Still, I denied myself the time to listen, and I remained on the hamster wheel until my two awakenings.

When I finally got it that I had been ignoring my inner voice, a wave of mixed feelings washed over me. First, sadness for having ignored my inner voice, and then a feeling of gratitude and hope. I made peace with the sadness and committed to reconnecting with my inner voice. I was excited to get to know "her" and to hear all that she had to tell me. I found her to be a wise best friend who always had my best interests in mind and at heart.

I set aside time daily to check in and listen. At first, it was ten minutes each morning to see what I was feeling and needing. I literally asked my inner self, "What are you feeling?" "What do you do need?" I asked each question three times and quietly waited for my inner voice to answer. These early sessions felt awkward. *Am I doing this right? Am I making up the messages? Is what I'm hearing true?* I began to trust what I heard and felt without question. I was building a muscle. I wrote down what came to me, and the messages felt right. Have you ever felt that something was right but you couldn't intellectually say why? That's how it was for me.

I expanded my sessions of quiet listening time. I took myself into deeper meditation to connect with my inner self beyond my intuition to my higher self. I began to feel joy and peace in my body. I began by consciously pausing and taking several deep breaths. As I continued to breathe, I dropped my awareness into my core, then my hips, thighs, and into the soles of my feet. This grounded me with Mother Earth. I drew in her energy from deep in the center of the earth, and my body filled with brightness and vitality. I visualized the energy to be so strong that it traveled out past my body and filled the room. I created this container for myself to hear what my higher self had to say.

In this spaciousness, I continued to breathe as I visualized stepping into the middle of a huge, empty container. I saw it as an open bowl as big as a football stadium. There I felt safe, open, and expansive. Then I did something amazing. I listened! My body felt peacefully open, and I simply sat and LISTENED. I felt no rush, and had no anxiety. I was 100% present. When random mind chatter popped in, I acknowledged it and then I let it go with another deep breath. In most of these early days, I had no agenda other than to listen for what came up. Any message I received I quickly recorded in my journal that sat patiently on my lap. I'd open my eyes half way, quickly but calmly write the message, then close my eyes again to listen for more. I continued this process until I felt complete.

> *My listening became effortless, and I started*
> *to crave this time with my inner self.*

It felt expansive to sit and listen. The experience was truly a night-and-day difference from all of the thinking and strategizing that had been my habit. I felt a peace that I had never experienced before. I listened effortlessly, and I started to crave this time with my inner self. Some days I could hardly jump into my comfy chair fast enough to reconnect with my inner life. My private sanctuary, my very own guru with my best interests at heart, was there 24/7, just for me. What a comfort was that knowing!

I began to ask open-ended questions as I listened. I'd focus on my business or personal life to see if there were issues I needed guidance on. I asked questions about developing my product, navigating an issue in my divorce, and finding clarity around a limiting story I continued to carry. During this process, I felt joyful and peaceful. I felt completely safe, loved, and supported in my favorite overstuffed chair, my legs crossed, a blanket on my lap, and my favorite journal quickly filling up with deep insights and next steps for my life. It was a little shocking—who would have known Inner Listening could be so amazing?

After building a strong practice to ground myself and connect with my intuition, I began practicing the exercise at my desk before working on the next phase of product development, and especially before any work on my divorce proceedings. Astounding things began to happen. Next steps and solutions appeared. The more I grounded myself, the more I was able to feel and hear my intuitive voice throughout my day.

When new opportunities or issues came my way, instead of getting in my head and trying to figure them out logically, I dropped my awareness into my body to connect with my higher self, my intuition. *What did I feel? Was I aligned with my truth? Did I feel any resistance?* I got really good at being curious about my feelings, and I stopped judging what came up. Instead I adopted a perspective that whatever came up, regardless if it was a strong negative or positive emotion, I would view it as information to be listened to. It was information that either empowered me or held me back. Either way, it was perfect information to receive an action on. To this day, I continue to enjoy and deepen my practice of listening. Let's dive deeper into the act of Inner Listening. This Power of Radiant Achievement can have a tremendous impact on your life for very little effort.

Activating and strengthening your Power of Inner Listening requires a practice of mindful awareness.

There is no one right or best way to listen. Below are a few of the practices I used and continue to use to keep me connected to my inner voice (my intuition and higher self). I encourage you to try all of them and decide which works best for you. In the beginning, you may feel awkward, or you may think you aren't hearing anything. Be patient and keep at it. It may take some time.

1. **Practice living in the present moment.** In order to activate and strengthen your Power of Inner Listening, you need to

be conscious and aware during your day. If you don't already have a practice of mindfulness, now is the time to commit to it. The fastest and easiest way to be mindful is to focus on the present moment—NOW. Now is the time and place from which your intuition and higher self speak. Focus on the past or the future makes it impossible to use your Power of Inner Listening. Just notice where your attention is and consciously bring it back to the present moment.

2. **Schedule daily quiet time to listen.** Start with a short block of time, five or ten minutes. It is helpful to schedule your practice for the same time each day, as that will more easily become a habit. You may find it beneficial to set a timer. For me, a timer allowed me to totally let go and not worry about being "gone" too long. Find a comfortable place to sit without being interrupted. I don't recommend lying down, as it's too easy to fall asleep. Once you are settled in your quiet space, close your eyes and take some slow, deep breaths. Feel your body slow down. Focus on the fullness of your inhale and exhale. With each breath, slow down your brain and body even more. Feel into the openness of the moment by sensing the open space around you. You can sense this openness by feeling the space immediately around you, the space around you in the room you are sitting in, and the space around you in the universe.

After several deep breaths, ask yourself "What am I feeling?" Then sit and listen. Whatever you feel or hear from your body, acknowledge it and write it down. Thank your body for giving you its message. Keep doing this until the timer goes off. If nothing comes up that's okay; continue breathing slowly in and out. After a few breaths, ask the question again and then listen. It's okay if thoughts pop up. Simply acknowledge them and let them go. If it's tough to let a thought go, imagine putting it on a lily pad and let it go on an imaginary flowing river. Remember, the key part of this exercise is to connect with your body. To give you additional support, I have created short centering meditation that you can access as part of the bonus material in the Radiant Achiever App. (See the end of the chapter for details on how to access this.)

3. **Do a deep-dive meditation on a specific subject, such as your callings, your business or a key relationship, including your relationship with yourself.** Ground yourself as you did in step 1 above. Then, call in your intuition, your higher self. Ask for guidance as you sit in this wide-open container of receptivity. Speak your question out loud with wonder and curiosity. "I wonder how..." or "I wonder what..." opens your receptivity better than, for example, "Why...?" Sit patiently and listen. This is the starting point of a beautiful journey. Keep at it and reach out for assistance as needed. As in step 1 above, record everything that bubbles to the surface. Do not judge or analyze it in the moment. Capture it and reflect on it afterward.

4. **Be conscious and aware of how you receive your messages.** Remember, your intuition is always talking to you, both internally and externally. Stay present and aware when you hear a message that floats in (as opposed to a deliberate thought). Acknowledge the message, pay attention to it, and thank your inner wisdom for delivering it to you in perfect timing. When you consciously see and acknowledge these messages, you are saying, "Thank you and more please!" You are, in effect, building your Inner Listening muscle, and the stronger that muscle, the more you open yourself to creativity, synchronicity, grace, and ease.

Here are some examples of when your intuition might speak to you:

- when you are talking with someone, personally or professionally;
- when you are reading;
- when you are listening to music;
- when you are working to solve a problem;
- when you are triggered by something you feel strongly about;
- when you are being playful;
- when you are out in nature.

A Pause for Reflection: Understanding Your Embodiment of the POWER OF INNER LISTENING

In this reflection, you can examine your own experience and embodiment of your Power of Inner Listening. Grab your journal. Find a quiet place to sit and listen without interruption. Take a couple of deep breaths to get centered and to connect with your inner wisdom. When you are ready, write your responses to the following questions:

1. *In what ways do I see my Power of Inner Listening in action?*

2. *In what ways have I been limiting or ignoring my connection and trust in my Power of Inner Listening?*

3. *What next step can I take to more consciously utilize my Power of Inner Listening?*

BONUS MATERIAL

Enter "800008" in the Radiant Achiever APP TRACK NOW page to unlock additional content related to this chapter.

CHAPTER 6

The Power of Inspired Action

The Power of Inspired Action promotes wonder and curiosity and creates an environment for synchronicity to occur.

Pursuit of any goal requires action. Depending on the size of the goal, we may take hundreds or even thousands of small actions on the path toward accomplishment. We often identify and track these steps with a strategy or project plan. I was a huge user of very detailed project plans in both my personal and professional life for years. If you are like I was, your strategic plan is likely created from a place of logic, which uses primarily your left brain.

A common method that many of us have learned and had reinforced, both in our personal and professional lives, is to look at our goal and break it down into smaller chunks. I spent years in Information Technology, planning and executing big systems projects, which required detailed plans to support time and budget goals. This traditional model of achievement leaves little room for Inspired Action. In fact, there is no place on a project plan for Inspired Action. A carefully created plan of milestones, tasks, and to-dos may be logical, but it blocks the potential of the Power of Inspired Action as a goal achievement tool.

The *just do it* mentality has us acting as machines—look at the task or project plan and *just do* the next thing. It's a mechanical process that, if taken to its extreme, thwarts any chance for fun, serendipity, and I'll even go so far as to say, the magical moments

RADIANT ACHIEVEMENT

that come from tapping into the Power of Inspired Action. I am not saying project plans are wrong, bad, or unnecessary. Like everything, there is a time and place for strategic plans AND Inspired Actions. It is not either or; rather, it's both.

Radiant Achievement, by its nature, allows your desires to manifest in a balanced and fluid way. Inspired Action creates this fluid environment. When you are inspired to act, the path toward your goal unfolds serendipitously, right before your eyes. When you see this happen time and again, you will realize that you don't need to have everything figured out before you take action. Activating and engaging the Power of Inspired Action brings excitement and ease to the achievement of your goal and opens you up to support from the Universe. My intention is to open your eyes and heart to an expanded and up-leveled view of goal achievement that creates space for magic to happen.

Let's dive into the Power of Inspired Action and see how it fits into the pursuit of your soul-centered calling, as well as more mainstream goals.

When you receive guidance to move forward with an Inspired Action, you feel an internal YES.

Simply said, Inspired Action is doing something that you feel *inspired* to do. The Power of Inspired Action is your ability to discern and act upon the inspirations you receive. How do you know an action is inspired? Inspired Actions connect with your intuition. You feel an internal *yes* when you hear or consider the action. This internal *yes* can be a gut feeling, where you simply know it is the next thing to do. Or it may come as a message through spoken or written word.

The message can come from your intuition or inner knowing, or it can come through an external source. External sources are everywhere. I have experienced Inspired Actions in the form of phone call, emails, face-to-face conversations, and even from listening to a podcast. I have heard of people passing a random billboard that contained a message to call someone. That might sound crazy, but I see this as a fascinating synchronicity. The Universe is always speaking to us, and it's up to us to hear these messages by staying open and aware.

Regardless of how you receive Inspired Action, the feelings are the same. You have a sense that this IS something to do, either immediately or in the near future, that moves you towards your goal. Inspired Action comes in different shapes and sizes. It may be something as small as making a phone call, or something bigger, like signing up for Toastmasters, creating a business plan, or taking a trip to Africa. You can be inspired to be more creative or to be more structured and strategic. I experienced that in the early months of 2020. After a couple of highly creative years, my inner voice said it's time to put all that I have created into more structured action regarding my coaching and programs. *YES!* I felt deeply aligned with that message and am now on a path of creativity and strategy.

This showcases that Inspired Action, if you let it, will gently guide you to your next steps. When you engage this power, you don't have to think hard or struggle to come up with the right next step. The Power of Inspired Action removes any self-pressure to be perfect and mistake-proof. Instead, you enjoy the benefit of moving fluidly and gracefully toward your goal. Over time, you will experience a broader benefit of taking consistent Inspired Action. You will come to trust these inspirations, you will learn that things can happen with ease and grace, and you will experience positive movement toward your goal without knowing ahead of time exactly how your action will affect your intended goal. I have heard time and again from clients and friends who surrendered to their Inspired Action how amazed they were at the results and the easy progress toward their goal. Sometimes they discover an entirely new path; other times there is profound learning; and always there is unexpected joy. I experienced (and continue to experience) all of this and more!

RADIANT ACHIEVEMENT

When I decided to follow the inspiration rather than fight it, my life took on a new orientation and energy.

A few years prior to my awakenings, I had been in the habit of needing everything figured out before I took action toward my goals. I acted mostly from my thoughts and my fears of failing or looking foolish. It was one thing to let my inspiration guide me for throwing a dinner party; but I couldn't allow that for my heart-centered goals. My ego was fragile back then, and I couldn't take the chance of being ridiculed or judged. I feared it would crush me and stop me from ever opening my heart to my dreams in the future.

After my awakenings, as I reconnected with my Inner Listening, I began to hear small intuitive messages—things like "go walk on the beach" or "sit with a cup of tea." Consciously I decided not to question what I heard. Rather, I followed it, and I learned an entirely new orientation to my daily activities. It initially felt odd to act this way, but it also felt aligned with my energy and my feelings and needs in the moment. Whether I was feeling sunshine on my face and cool water tickling my toes or tasting the hot sweetness of rose hip tea, each action filled me in its own way. I acknowledged during my walk or as I sipped tea how wonderful I felt. Afterward, I told myself I was glad I listened to that voice, because it was exactly what I needed.

One time, I was inspired simultaneously to take a beach walk and to invite a girlfriend. I called my friend, who quickly accepted— she had been about to go for a beach walk, herself. Perfect timing. We had a fabulous, deep talk during our walk, something I would have missed had I not listened to that voice inspiring me to head to the beach. That's the Power of Inspired Action—a result better than I could have imagined. And that result led to another big shift regarding Inspired Actions.

The more Inspired Action I took, the more I LET GO of expecting a certain outcome. I began to see that I don't need to know what the outcome will be. I consciously shifted my mindset to believe that, while I have an idea for a desired outcome, it is important to be open to something even better. This mental shift made it faster and easier to act on the tasks that came to me during my listening sessions. I built a trust in what I was receiving, and I became comfortable not knowing how all the pieces would fit together. I accepted that I was being presented with a piece of the puzzle and that I should follow through on it.

One such moment came when my Mantra Makeup Mat™ website was being built. This website would ultimately share my story, represent my product brand, and inspire women to create a morning ritual for themselves using my product. I felt such pressure to get this right! Have you ever put that pressure on yourself? One morning while sitting at my cherished desk, I saw "create website outline" on the top of my to-do list. My gut wrenched, and I felt fearful as I fidgeted to start this big action. I started with a blank piece of paper, intending to draw out how I wanted the website to look, feel, and sound. A blank piece of paper was a scary thing for me back then. How would I get this website figured out? I felt fear and resistance. That combo was an old, familiar trigger of me wanting to know (maybe you know this one too) and feeling certain that I wouldn't be able to figure it out, now or easily. I focused with my analytical mind for direction and information, and my fear of not knowing screamed even louder.

With just enough presence of mind, I caught myself about to go down a rabbit hole of *how* that would keep me stuck all day. That was the old me, who lived with the systematic model of achievement and needed to know how it would all go. But this was not me now. I had inner powers to use. I took a couple of deep breaths and relaxed my body and my brain. I closed my eyes, took another deep breath, and *aha!* It came to me like a flash across the sky—I needed to be in a place of wonder and curiosity about my website.

Put yourself in a receptive state for Inspired Actions by consciously using the prompt "I wonder."

I scribbled across the top of my blank sheet of paper, "I wonder," and I brainstormed ways to fill in the blank. *I wonder what layout I could use? I wonder how I can show the key features of the product? I wonder who can take the product pictures? I wonder what types of video I can include? I wonder what colors to use? I wonder what to include about me? I wonder what I can say about my story?* I sat for some time, totally immersed in free-flowing brainstorm mode. When I felt complete with my inquiry, I counted up the number of topics, and there were more than 25 *I wonder* questions. Wow! I was amazed at what came out during this 15-minute session. It felt great to see all those thoughts on paper; but it was even more exciting to connect with the depth and variety of topics that emerged. Many of the ideas I had not even thought of before, yet they magically came from my brainstorm time. I see now that I had tapped into a deeper place of consciousness than my ego or analytical mind would have allowed. I was energized, and my initial fear was completely gone.

I reread the list and felt drawn to the first statement: "I wonder what layout I could use?" "Hmmm, that is a great topic," I said. "One that is the cornerstone of the entire website development process." The next thought that popped up for me was, "I wonder who can help me figure out the layout?" As soon as I said that statement out loud, I heard, "Email your virtual assistant." Of course. She was the perfect place to start. So, my Inspired Actions came first from my brainstorm list, and then my intuition guided me. I jumped into action and emailed my virtual assistant. Before I knew it, I had specific direction about actions to help define my website layout. Not only was I unstuck, I had a list of terrific questions to move me through the entire website design process. I have used the *I wonder* process dozens of times now, and it works *wonders* to move me into Inspired Action.

The Universe will serendipitously deliver Inspired Actions when you consciously remain open and aware to powers greater than yourself.

I want to share with you the most significant shift in how I sometimes receive my Inspired Actions: They are delivered by the Universe! I love acknowledging and acting on these fun, serendipitous moments.

In the fall of 2016, I attended a conference where I had the privilege of connecting with the wonderfully wise Jean Houston. One thing she said that stuck with me is, "When you pay attention to the Universe, the Universe pays attention to you." I had never thought about the Universe in this way. That message was key for me to hear and embody. After I left the workshop, I paid closer attention to everything that came my way—in my emails, in conversations with people, while I was running errands. I believed that the Universe communicated with me through these channels. It wasn't that I was looking for something, but rather staying connected to the messages that came my way and paying close attention to the ones that resonated with me.

Something very interesting occurred. I started to see answers and next steps for my business. One particular time, I was looking to get my product more fully into the community. I received a random email regarding a Black Friday pop-up shopping event at a local outdoor shopping center. Perfect! I had been thinking of finding a holiday shopping vendor opportunity, and there it was, right in my inbox. It came effortlessly, simply by reading my email subject lines. I opened the email and read the details. It was a perfect fit for what I wanted to do. I emailed the organizer, and within a few days I was set up as an official vendor for the event. With a big smile on my face, I sat and reflected on how quickly and easily this had all unfolded.

Several months later, a business associate suggested I keep track of all the serendipitous happenings I was experiencing. The idea resonated with me, because things were happening so frequently that I could hardly remember all the magical unfoldings. I started a new journal just for this, and what occurred on some days was almost comical. I would write a short talk, and then phone calls would come with invitations to speak. I clarified my new brand, and phone calls and emails came from people looking for a life coach. Three different men asked me out, though I had never made the effort of registering with a dating website. In fact, my logical brain had said I wasn't ready to date, but my intuition (and the Universe) had bigger plans for me. That is the power of connection with universal energy.

I see Inspired Action as a gift from our higher self and the Universe. If you don't feel that you have a conscious connection to universal energy, I encourage you to expand your perspective. The Universe is here to help, if you are open to receiving its guidance. I have come to trust and act on the Inspired Actions that come to me. As a result, my journey toward achieving my personal and professional goals and dreams has been fun and exciting in ways I never could have imagined. When I look back at my old habit of systematic achievement, I remember that it wasn't fun or exciting. It was a lot of H-A-R-D W-O-R-K, and even a fair amount of suffering from all the thinking, second guessing, and over planning. That all changed when I opened to powers beyond my personal power.

Activating and strengthening your connection with the Power of Inspired Action requires some inner shifts.

Activating and strengthening your ability to take Inspired Action requires you to BE and THINK differently. Making these core shifts allows you to more easily HEAR the Inspired Actions that come to you and then to ACT on them. Like all the other powers, you are born with this power. If you don't feel strongly connected to it, it's not because you don't have it; you simply need to reconnect with it and strengthen it. It's fun to develop this power! Here are several suggestions for trusting this power and receiving its gifts:

1. **Be open to your Inspired Actions coming from ANYWHERE.** And I mean anywhere! In addition to being inspired to actions through my intuition, I have been inspired through emails messages, from conversations with

people, from overhearing people's conversations on a bus or plane, from a magazine article or headline, and from podcasts (I get this one a lot). Consciously adopt the mindset that Inspired Action is all around you. Make the inner shift to see and believe that the entire Universe supports you to achieve your goal and the Universe guides you to Inspired Action all throughout your day.

2. **Be open to answers or steps that are better than you could think of on your own.** This was a big relief for me! I put so much pressure on myself to come up with the "right," "smart," "efficient," or "effective" next step. When you open yourself to universal intelligence, you tap into an unlimited field of wisdom that yields ideas and next steps you would not otherwise think of on your own. Know you are wise, and also know there are powers wiser than you to connect with and receive benefit from.

3. **Trust the *yes* when it occurs.** Trusting the *yes* may require you to give up the belief that the "right" answers are logical. Step out of your left brain and trust beyond what you think. Trust your gut, trust the knowing that comes with the hit of an Inspired Action. When you receive an Inspired Action, don't get logical or analytical trying to figure out if you should do it. Step out in faith and trust and take the action by staying connected with the feeling of *yes*.

4. **Be open to where Inspired Action may lead you.** Our project plans teach us that we need to know how our next steps fit together. We've been conditioned to have to see how the plan will unfold. Instead, be okay with uncertainty. Shift to the idea that Inspired Action is a key part of any goal and that by not expecting a specific outcome, we open ourselves to a path that is more exciting, more effective, more joyful, and more growth-oriented. Even if you can't see exactly how this action fits into your journey toward your

goal, stay open that it will lead you to exactly where you are supposed to be.

5. **Discover Inspired Actions by stepping into the creativity of *I wonder*.** Just as you might go to the gym and consciously lift weights to build muscles, you can use an *I wonder* brainstorm session to build your Power of Inspired Action muscle. Set a timer for five or ten or fifteen minutes and get curious. *I wonder how..., I wonder in what ways..., I wonder who....* Curiosity is a simple and effective way to build your inner muscle of receiving Inspired Actions. Once you have your brainstorm list, read it and feel into which action most energizes you. Take immediate action on whatever energizes you most, no matter how small. Your actions are cumulative and will build on each other.

A Pause for Reflection: Understanding Your Embodiment
of the POWER OF INSPIRED ACTION

In this reflection, you can explore your own experience and embodiment of your Power of Inspired Action. Grab your journal. Find a quiet place to sit and listen without interruption. Take a couple of deep breaths to get centered and to connect with your inner wisdom. When you are ready, write your responses to the following questions:

1. *In what ways do I see the Power of Inspired Action at play in my life?*

2. *In what ways have I been limiting or ignoring my connection and trust in the Power of Inspired Action?*

3. *What next step can I take to more consciously use my Power of Inspired Action?*

BONUS MATERIAL

Enter "800009" in the Radiant Achiever APP TRACK NOW page to unlock additional content related to this chapter.

CHAPTER 7

The Power of Commitment

Believing in someone else's dream is often easier than committing to our own desires and callings.

Have you ever noticed how easy it is to commit to something or someone external to you, like your community, a charity, your kids, your partner, or your boss? Are you a perpetual cheerleader, offering support and encouragement to everyone around you, but finding it difficult to support (and commit to) yourself and your goals, desires, and calling? Do you frequently say, "It's not that big a deal to cancel my plans," in favor of another person's wants that move them toward THEIR goals, desires, and callings? I get it. We are nurturers by nature. On top of that, many of us have been conditioned that we should give, give, give. Many of us (me included) were not taught how to commit to our own needs while also supporting the needs of others. We were taught either/or—either I am here to help you or I am here to help myself.

In the moment, it feels good to support someone else, but when we consistently put our own plans/ideas/dreams on hold because "they aren't that big of a deal," we damage our heart and soul. Maybe that sounds harsh, but effectively that behavior says we aren't as worthy as the other person. It says they are more important than we are. Wrapped up in this may be fears of speaking our voice, fears around conflict, fears of taking a stand for what we believe or want. Self-denial is a protection mechanism that keeps us momentarily in the comfort zone. When we think, "I don't want to rock the boat," or, "What if others don't support me," we protect our heart from disappointment and, at the same time, deny our truth. Ultimately, we sacrifice living our highest potential. I know this to be true, because I lived like that for many years.

When I went through my awakenings and healing, I learned new things that supported my journey to step into my truth. I gained a new understanding and appreciation for my Power of Commitment. In order to feel fulfilled in this lifetime, to courageously stay the course to YOUR highest potentials, to honor your soul calling, you must build your inner muscle of Commitment to Y-O-U! That means committing to your higher self, not your ego. In fact, you may need to put your ego in the back seat in order to fully step into your personal Power of Commitment.

Let's get on the same page regarding the Power of Commitment and how it fits into the Radiant Achievement paradigm.

Commitment means resolving to pursue your calling, dream, or desire no matter what it takes.

Commitment means you are dedicated with every fiber of your being to achieve what your soul desires. Commitment exists in your body first. It is a visceral experience, one that you feel in your gut or your heart or, as I experienced, as a knowing in your entire body. Commitment exists first as a deep feeling that then inspires intellectual commitment. This full-body *yes* says you will pursue your goal no matter what—no matter how you get there and no matter how long it takes. It isn't about killing yourself or losing everything to achieve a goal. That is the old paradigm around Commitment and achievement. The Commitment of which I speak is internally focused, and it supports a transformation that allows you to do whatever it takes to achieve your calling.

We've often heard that you can't solve your problems with the same thinking that created them. The same applies to committing to achieving your calling. Manifesting your goal or desire requires some inner and outer changes. Those changes look different for each person, but let's address some common themes. Externally, it means willingness to make space in your life to pursue your goal. It means stop doing some things and start doing some other things. I found myself saying *no* more often as I stepped more fully into my calling. I didn't feel sad about it. My Commitment to do what my soul was so loudly calling me to felt empowering.

One useful shift is the willingness to take action that is good enough versus needing it to be perfect. I never considered myself a perfectionist until I started putting my voice out there in print and videos. Boy, did I feel the need to get it perfect! I worked and struggled for hours, laboring over just the right words. We need to commit to doing our best in the present moment and know that we will expand and grow as we continue to practice.

Another key change for me (and many achievers) was committing even when it was uncomfortable. I say it often to myself and my clients: "Get comfortable being uncomfortable!" As we get older and our habits and patterns are deeply ingrained, it's less and less appealing to step outside our comfort zone. We become creatures of comfort. As warm and cozy as that feels, it is not a place of growth. When we step in to follow our calling, when we dare to bring our authentic self into the world, new and unfamiliar situations feel uncomfortable. Isn't that great? Get used to that. Being uncomfortable means you are living on your growing edge and that you are continuing to expand and grow as you pursue you calling. For years, I lived inside my external comfort zone, even though inside I felt like I was slowly dying. Now I am so okay being uncomfortable as I lean in to my growing edge.

To commit to my callings, I first had to commit to ME.

Before my awakening, as a wife and mother, I wholeheartedly felt a calling to support and uplift my husband and children to achieve their highest calling. I subconsciously believed that supporting them limited my time and energy to pursue my own fulfillment. So, I put my personal and professional needs and desires at the bottom of my priority list. My first dedication was to my husband to build his career. If that meant I planned a dinner party, packed his clothes for a business trip, attended a function, took care of the cars, made vacation plans, and coordinated home projects, then that is what I did. I added to that mix my Commitment of time and energy to my children's academic and athletic pursuits. I was the team mom, non-profit board member, classroom volunteer, driver, cheerleader, and party planner.

I struggled to create a balance of Commitments to others without losing Commitments to myself. In many respects, I failed myself. I had few, if any, boundaries regarding my time and energy. If I was tired, I'd have another cup of coffee. If something came up that affected one of my Commitments or appointments, I'd cancel my event to support my family. Initially, this felt good. Over time, I felt resentful and even heartbroken, because I knew I was making myself and my needs unimportant.

I feel that God and my angels looked over me and supported me. Every so often during my marriage, I would get these random inspirations. When I look back, I see the trail of triggering events (hindsight is 20/20, as they say), but that's insignificant now. Periodically (sometimes years apart), I got an idea, and with it a strong feeling that I HAD to follow through on it. I believe God handed me these experiences every so often to remind me that I am more than a cheerleader and support person for my family. These inspirations included my callings to compete in fitness-related figure competitions, to travel for a real family vacation to enjoy hiking and snorkeling together, and to redefine my career as a coach and entrepreneur. My calling to leave the corporate world and launch my own life-coaching business was one of the most significant callings I have answered and one of the most transformational Commitments I have ever made.

To commit to this calling, I first had to commit to me. Not only in my body, but also externally with my company (at the time) and, especially, with my family. Going out on a limb to risk hearing *no* was scary for me. I had to be prepared to stand up for me. Fortunately, I received a *yes* from everyone, even if it wasn't as enthusiastic as the *YES* I felt in my body.

Embarking on my entrepreneurial journey was thrilling. After the first couple weeks the stars faded, and the reality of my choice began to unfold. I got glimpses of what I would need to do and who I would need to become in order to achieve my dream of being a highly successful coach. Could I stay committed to a schedule? Could I talk with people about their struggles to achieve their goals? Could I really help people transform their lives? Sometimes I felt scared, stopped in my tracks. Other times my body came alive, expanding my belief in myself. Discomfort, uncertainty, doubts, and fears accompanied me on my journey to manifest my business dream. Yet, I knew this was part of the journey, and not a reason to bail on my Commitment to myself and my goal. My fears, problems, and blocks were gracious gifts and opportunities to grow, expand, and become my fullest self.

Committing to my smaller goals moved me down the path to say YES to the bigger callings that came later.

Staying committed to achieve my calling opened a doorway to personal growth and fulfillment. I progressively opened up to experience and develop parts of myself that I hadn't known existed. That, in turn, unlocked deeper parts of me that I had not previously experienced or expressed. I expanded from working one-on-one with clients to working with groups. I expanded again to include speaking engagements, to build a tribe, and to connect with readers and clients via my blog and monthly newsletter. Saying *yes* and committing to my smaller goals moved me down the path to say *yes* to my bigger callings (like writing this book) that would come in the future, especially those that came after my awakenings.

The Commitment, growth, and fulfillment I experienced from pursuing my early callings unconsciously mixed with my remnants of heartache from previously denying my desires. This was fertile soil for me to transform how I committed to myself after my awakenings. I experienced an especially pivotal day that forever changed my level of Commitment to myself.

My pivotal day was one of deep reflection, tears, and pain. I deeply ached, not from the loss of my marriage, but from a more serious loss—the loss of my self-worth and self-love. My feeling of pain and sorrow was palpable. My body felt weak as I sat slumped in my favorite chair. My head hung down, and I watched the tears drip, drip, drip onto my pajamas that I just couldn't get out of that day. I had forsaken myself. I had denied ME, time and time again. Deeply pained, I looked into the eyes of my inner child, who was feeling unloved and abandoned by me.

Even as my tears flowed, I sensed this was part of my healing. I was releasing my pushed-down hurt and shame. If I kept my emotions bottled up, I would remain stuck and create a breeding ground for future problems. So, I let it out—the tears, the sobbing, the strained breaths in and out as my nose had become so stuffed from crying. I knew I would be okay. I knew I was not alone. God was with me, watching over me. At one point, as my emotions calmed down, I visualized myself climbing into God's lap, curled up like a little girl on her father's lap for a nap. Curled up and cozy, I let out a sigh. I thanked God for being there for me and for keeping me safe. After my rest on His lap I asked Him to take my pain away. In my mind, I handed Him my pain of not loving myself and not owning my worth. Then I handed Him my pain for all the times I didn't take a stand for me, the times I disrespected myself, the times I allowed others to disrespect me. He lovingly took these pains and released them into the river of life.

RADIANT ACHIEVEMENT

Drawing a line in the sand, I committed to wholeheartedly love myself and unapologetically pursue the callings of my soul.

When I opened my eyes from this visualization, I felt cleansed, lighter, and at peace. I sat with these happier feelings and continued to breathe them into my body. With each deep breath in, peace filled me. With a slow breath out, I connected with the lightness of my body. What a beautiful moment! I felt a new love for myself, for all parts of me—for the little girl inside me who was funny and playful; for the adult woman who was intelligent, capable, and creative; for the wise woman in me filled with infinite potential and the keeper of my deeper callings. I felt authentic love for each part of me, and something new welled up in me—a new calling filled with energy, hope, and promise. The calling was for a new *lifetime* Commitment. I was called to commit to me, and I said *YES!* Sitting in my favorite chair, in my pajamas, with tears drying on my cheeks, I committed that for the rest of my life I would wholeheartedly love me and unapologetically pursue the callings of my soul.

The line I drew in the sand that day gave my Commitments entirely new meaning. Each Commitment was a *yes* to me - to my growth, to my fulfillment, and to my contribution in the world. Since then, I have made hundreds of full-body Commitments, big and small. When I committed to bring my creative idea to life (the Mantra Makeup Mat™), I felt deep peace. I KNEW with 100% certainty that my idea would come to life in perfect time, and I was open to how it would unfold. I was not attached to a particular timeframe or path. And it happened! My vision came to life in the fall of 2016.

My total Commitment to me doesn't mean it's always easy to choose me or that I always do choose me first. I am still working to balance numerous roles. I no longer have young children and a husband at home, but I do have important people and facets of my life to engage with. My kids have launched their lives and I am single, but I have as many roles as before; they're simply different.

Now I am a grandma and dog-mom to a senior dog who's had health issues. Now I am a BFF like I haven't been since college! I'm also a student, a dancer, and yes, an entrepreneur.

In my early days of transformation, I often denied or delayed my desires for no reason other than old habit. Commitment to myself required me to step up and see myself as equal to everyone else in my life. I shifted my perspective: Following my callings and dreams was my fullest expression of me; didn't I want to give myself and everyone I interact with the fullest version of me? Of course! So, with my friends and family, I stick to my Commitments to me. I periodically rearrange things so I can do both the grandma thing and the business thing. I get a dog sitter without feeling the guilt I felt in the past. I pass on a social event when I am approaching a deadline, and I know my friendship won't end because of it. In fact, just the opposite!

Now I encourage my adult kids versus telling them what to do and how to live. I am fully present with my friends and family, because my time with them is my conscious choice, not out of obligation. The same holds true for my work. I don't have that inner pull any more. In each of my roles, including my role of self, I elect to pursue what matters most to me in a blend that feels good in my heart. Am I perfect at this? No. But I am committed to continuing to be me in every moment and to honor my inner callings as much as I honor all my other roles. Life is a journey. Things ebb and flow. As long as I remember that, I can connect with and flow with the big picture of my life.

***The Power of Commitment is, at the highest level,
a Commitment to living a fulfilling life.***

Commitment is key to your Radiant Achievement, because when you say *yes* to achieving your goal, you are really saying *yes* to YOU. Your inner callings are the seeds of your Radiance and, ultimately, your fulfillment. At the highest level, you are committing to live your fullest life. You are a being with infinite potential, ideas, gifts, and contributions, and Commitment to YOU is a lifelong journey.

When you commit at this deeper level, you simultaneously commit to who you need to BE to achieve your goal. Becoming is a combination of inner and outer work. It's much more than actions and tasks. Commitment to the inner work means adjusting your mindset, letting go of old disempowering stories, being more open and vulnerable. The list of inner work never ends, and that means we always have room for growth and personal evolution. The specific Commitments you need to make will reveal themselves if you stay open to see and receive them.

Committing to do whatever it takes, committing to inner work requires us to let go of old ways of being, old beliefs and stories. This includes how we think and feel about ourself, about others, and the world. Recognizing our beliefs, our self-talk, and our habits reveals what we have attracted up to now. To manifest something different, we need to shift our self-talk, our habits, and our beliefs to line up with what we want to create. Inner work requires love, compassion, and honesty. The perspective that letting go of the old ways allows you to become more of your authentic self supports you to move through change with less struggle or resistance.

For me, the Power of Commitment created a focus and inner perseverance that I hold from a deep place. It gives me trust in my future that allows me to step boldly into each of my callings. That's a powerful stance! Know that your desires were given to you for a reason, even if you can't clearly see the reason right now. Honor and pursue these callings at some point, somehow, and in some way. It's not a race, but rather an inner and outer journey to express what is integral for you. Be excited to see where committing to your calling leads you.

The Power of Commitment keeps you on course in uncertain times, keeps you confident and relaxed even when things are uncomfortable. Questions will come up. The path may be hazy.

Some turns may lead to a dead end; simply backtrack or start over. When you commit to a soul-centered journey, you are not committing to perfection, to knowledge, or to a specific outcome. You are committing to listening, to stepping forward, to being inspired, to letting go, to starting up, to doing whatever you need to do.

One final gift from the Power of Commitment is the broadening of perspective about your goal. You can step back and see that pursuing and achieving your goal is not only for your benefit, but for the benefit of all who will be touched by your work. It moves your center from ME to US. It goes beyond achievement of a particular goal and moves you to your legacy, your divine impact. How you show up and who you are being impacts everyone you interact with. One group that you especially impact is children—your own children, children you work with in your profession, every child you interact with. Children are sponges and take what you say literally. Call them crazy, and they think they are crazy. Comment that they sing off key, and they may shrink from singing in public (that happened to me). I did my best to be a good mom when my kids were younger, but now I see how my need for control and having to figure it all out impacted them. I have apologized more than once for what I now see were my limiting beliefs that affected my parenting and interaction with them. NEVER underestimate your impact on someone's life, positive or negative. You will leave a legacy. What will it be?

Activating and strengthening your inner Power of Commitment is empowering and life-giving.

Pursuing Radiant Achievement doesn't mean forcing a Commitment; rather, your Commitment is empowered by an inner feeling of *yes*. Your full-body Commitment is your anchor as you take steps to achieve your goal. My clients and I have used several methods to strengthen our Power of Commitment. Try these:

1. **Write down your goal and refer to it often (preferably daily).** Feel the *yes* you felt when you first desired the goal. See yourself having already achieved the goal. Describe how it looks and feels when you achieve your calling. What are you doing? Where are you doing it? Who are you BEING as you live your calling? See deeply into this vision and bring it to life. The more vivid the detail, the stronger you will feel the achievement of your calling.

2. **Create space in your life to pursue your goal.** Look at your current "obligations." What can you stop doing? What can you start doing to support the achievement of your goal? Be realistic about how much time you are willing to dedicate NOW to pursuing your goal. Remember, this is not a race. You know your dream will manifest in its time, and it means devoting some time toward the goal, even if it's only one hour a week. Small progress over time strengthens your Commitment.

3. **If your goal seems too large right now, what smaller piece can you commit to?** Some callings from long ago I am now only realizing! Timing depends on how strong the calling feels now. Are you are called to step in for 100% focus and attention? Or do you feel you can only give it limited time for now? If your time is limited, find a smaller piece of the larger calling and make it so in a shorter timeframe and with less pressure. Our soul is not attached to how we move toward our calling; it only cares that we commit to something on that path. Start small and build from there.

4. **Identify and let go of old ways of being and thinking.** What limits you? Is it your stories about yourself, stories about abundance or about love? Is it something else? Listen to your self-talk and be aware of your actions. Ask yourself, "Is _____ holding me back or moving me toward my goal?" If it's not clearly moving you forward, then some part of it is limiting you. Do your inner work to identify and let

go of the disempowering belief. Use the process outlined in Chapter 4 about Mindset. It can be difficult to see our stories; be open to getting support.

5. **Take action that is good enough without needing to be perfect.** You lose connection to the momentum (and your Commitment) to your goal when you focus on perfection. Do your best in the moment and continue to step out, even if you don't feel fully prepared.

6. **Get comfortable being uncomfortable.** Commitment is not about comfort. Shifting into the mindset that you will be uncomfortable at times helps you stay committed to your goal. Doubts, fears, concerns, uncertainty, etc., are all part of the journey of pursuing your goal.

7. **Be okay with not knowing or seeing the entire path toward your goal.** Focus on the next best step. That is where your current Commitment lies. Commit to achieve the near-term actions, and trust that all actions will be accomplished in perfect timing.

A Pause for Reflection: Understanding Your
Embodiment of the POWER OF COMMITMENT

In this reflection, you will examine your own experience and embodiment of your Power of Commitment. Grab your journal. Find a quiet place to sit and listen without interruption. Take a couple of deep breaths to get centered and to connect with your inner wisdom. When you are ready, write your responses to the following questions:

1. **In what ways do I see the Power of Commitment in action in my life?**

2. **In what ways have I been limiting or ignoring my connection to the Power of Commitment?**

3. **What next step can I take to more consciously utilize the Power of Commitment?**

BONUS MATERIAL

Enter "800010" in the Radiant Achiever APP TRACK NOW page to unlock additional content related to this chapter.

CHAPTER 8

The Power of Reflection

In our fast-paced world, pausing to reflect may seem counter-productive, but it's one of our most productive tools.

In this GO, GO, GO society, we are absorbed in the DO, DO, DO of our lives. As a result, we often neglect the Power of Reflection. How many times have you heard yourself say, "I don't have time to stop and think," or, "I am so busy, I don't have enough time to get everything done." Overloaded task lists, over-scheduled days, and over-stressed mindsets (especially about time) all rob us of reflection time. Just like a car cannot continue to run without stops for gas, oil, and maintenance, we too need to pause, not just to refuel with food or sleep, but also to reflect. Keeping ourselves in drive all day until we drop, exhausted, onto the couch, bed, or chair evidences an epidemic of overwhelm, disconnection, and dis-ease. We are advanced technologically and medically, yet collectively we suffer more and more illness. One reason for this, I believe, is that we are not tapping into and using our inner Power of Reflection. Without realizing it, many people are living their lives backward.

The false belief that we lack time makes making an appointment to pause and be still (physically and mentally) unthinkable. We pause for Reflection in the midst of tasks, commitments, and unfinished business only when something goes wrong or when life takes an unexpected turn, as was the case for me.

I'm going to let you in on a little secret: The Power of Reflection will enhance your productivity in ways you may never have imagined. Doing more isn't what leads to achievement of your goal, dream, or calling. What brings results actually requires doing less and REFLECTING more. Are you shaking your head? Am I off my rocker? I, too, was once skeptical until I began to adopt a do-less-and-reflect-more lifestyle. By the end of this chapter, I hope you will see the value in the Power of Reflection and be excited to use it every day.

The Power of Reflection creates an energy that naturally pulls you toward your goal.

In its simplest form, the Power of Reflection is taking a mindful pause to shine a light on something by thinking, pondering, wondering, or celebrating. Reflecting lets you see and feel through the lens of your deeper intuition versus from your thinking brain. What do you think, ponder, wonder, and celebrate as you tap into your Power of Reflection? Anything in your life that you desire to give energy to! Let's distinguish between overthinking something (going around and around in your head, processing and reprocessing) and reflecting on something. The intention is different from one to the other.

The intention that supports the Power of Reflection is growth, learning, joy, love, care, empowerment. Essentially, we reflect for positive reasons. The overthinking loop is fraught with negativity— guilt, shame, or self-judgment. If you've been overthinking in this mode, I implore you to STOP. It doesn't serve you in any meaningful way, and it limits you from living a fulfilling life. The Power of Reflection is expansive and life giving. I would go as far as to say that using your Power of Reflection is an act of self-love. Does that sound amazing? If I can do something to show myself love, I want that. How about you?

Like all the powers, the Power of Reflection is not reserved for after you achieve your goal. You do it as part of your journey toward your goal. This is a shift of thinking for many. At one time, I believed that achieving goals, by definition, was hard, challenging, and exhausting. That is the old paradigm of systematic achievement and doesn't apply to Radiant Achievement. When you engage your Power of Reflection, you move toward your goal with less effort and more flow, grace, and ease. Instead of losing energy in the process, you gain momentum and energy.

In addition to its energetic properties, the Power of Reflection lets you course correct and redirect with grace and ease. Pursuing our inner callings is not like baking a cake or building a house. It involves uncharted waters, and as you move toward your vision you gather information, ideas, and new learnings. Some insights are so significant that they spark us to adjust our vision or plans. It's easier to adjust as we go along than to ignore our sense that something is off until it's excruciating to make a change. The Power of Reflection is key to our ability to sense, recognize, and adjust. We keep moving toward our calling, even when changes occur.

The Power of Reflection has another benefit. It keeps us aware and growing. With the positive intention of growth, we can see our successes and failures with non-judgmental awareness. We can see and feel subtle insights more quickly and easily than we otherwise would. Human beings can be very sensitive. It's hard to acknowledge our failures and shortcomings. It certainly was for me. When I began to use the Power of Reflection intentionally, I could let go of my oversensitivity and shift to an empowered mindset. Seeing and feeling both the good results and the areas that need improvement are critical to maintain forward momentum toward any size goal, dream, or calling. The Power of Reflection provides this and so much more.

The Power of Reflection keeps you present and connected to your unfolding journey.

Because Radiant Achievement is about the journey as well as your desired end result, engaging the Power of Reflection keeps you present and connected to what is unfolding. You stay connected to all the magical things that happen when you say *yes* to yourself and your dreams. Reflecting during the day and at the end of the day establishes a habit of mindful noticing.

You can reflect from multiple perspectives and for multiple purposes. One way is to reflect on your **outcomes**—from the day, from a project, from an event, or from a phone call. When you are in uncharted territory, Reflection helps you course correct as needed. Determine if the result is what you want. For instance, a part of your journey might be to put your message on social media and engage your audience. At the end of the day, reflect on the comments and feedback you received. *Did people resonate with my message? What types of comments and feedback did they leave? How might I engage more people?* Ask these questions as you reflect on the outcomes.

Another thing to reflect on is your **skills** and who you are being. Along your path, you are growing. If part of your journey requires you to sell your products, reflect on your sales results and how you showed up as a salesperson. You will see where your growing edge is on this leg of your journey. Your growing edge is that next area that is ripe for you to address and grow in. Reflection on your sales activity may reveal that you showed up with fear about making your offer. Making your offer without fear will be your growing edge. When you focus on only your growing edge versus the big vision, you can make small adjustments and not feel overwhelmed.

Something not so obvious is that noticing the **synchronicities** that occur in your day opens you wide for support from the Universe. Reflect on synchronicities! You are not alone on your journey. For this Reflection, ask: *What things seemed to happen magically? Did I have a conversation and suddenly receive an answer or a solution for something I've been working on? Was I invited to do something that I'd already been thinking of as a great next step?* These are synchronistic happenings; pay close attention to them. Feel life flowing and acknowledge the magic as the Universe supports you to achieve your goal.

One of the most powerful ways to reflect is to **celebrate**. I love to celebrate! Reflect on and celebrate key accomplishments, inner shifts, aha moments, ways you show up courageously, and first steps. Celebrate things that you let go of. Every day offers much to celebrate. Our mind is powerful, and when we focus on what we've successfully completed, we increase our forward momentum. Big and small accomplishments are all forward progress, and all of them deserve acknowledgment. It may feel silly to acknowledge the small things, like a phone call you made or a social media post you completed; however, I have found that our soul does not distinguish by the size of achievement. It only feels our gratitude for the accomplishment, and that registers internally as, "I would like to do more of this."

Acknowledge and value the insights you gained by putting into action the core learning of your Reflection. If you realize you have fears to address in your sales process, what next step can you take to address these fears? If you are not getting the desired engagement from your social media followers, what one thing can you do this week to address that? If you are celebrating a key accomplishment, who will you share that joy with? Acknowledgment enhances the energy of your Reflection and fuels progress toward your goal.

One type of Reflection was particularly instrumental in my growth and transformation. I learned this Reflection exercise from one of my mentors. It is especially impactful if you live in your head or feel like you are just going through the motions of life, because it reconnects you to your intuition and body wisdom. As with all Reflections, it helps to be grounded and centered before beginning. The intention of this Reflection is to connect with WHAT YOU FEEL and WHAT YOU NEED. How often do we feel something, but ignore or dismiss it as unimportant? We muscle on through our task and our day without paying attention to or honoring our feelings, until we are in crisis. Listen for what comes up when you ask your inner self, "What am I feeling?" Acknowledge and accept your answer. Validate your feelings without judgment, without trying to immediately fix it. Your relief and peace from acknowledging what you feel may surprise you.

The second part of this Power of Reflection exercise is to ask your inner self, "What do I need?" Then L-I-S-T-E-N, without thinking. When I first did this, I questioned what came up. Was it true? Was I making it up? If nothing comes up, ask the question again and patiently listen. You might hear a word or phrase, you might see an image, you might feel something in your body. Trust it. The more you ask these two questions, the more you strengthen your listening muscle. Be sure to acknowledge what comes up. I like to write it down and then feel into each item to see if any Inspired Action comes to me. I encourage you to do the same. One Inspired Action I received at least weekly was, "Take a nap." It made perfect sense; I was going through divorce proceedings, cancer treatment, and inner transformation. I was spending immense energy, and I needed the replenishment of sleep. I will admit that my connection to my Power of Reflection came to me the hard way. I definitely did not value it years earlier.

I stubbornly believed I didn't have time to reflect, which impacted how stressed I felt in my inner and outer world.

Before my awakenings, I lived in my head, often ignoring what I felt and needed. My only reflecting was to write in my journal about what made me mad or frustrated. My earliest Reflections go back to the mid-1990s, after my second child was born and I was working full-time and putting my husband through school. I carried heavy thoughts and feelings inside that I needed to process. I had way too much going on and way too many responsibilities. I felt unheard and abandoned. I was overwhelmed, lonely, and lacked the self-worth to share with my husband what I was going through and what I needed. I felt like a ticking time bomb about to explode. My only relief was to put things on paper. It was my only way to step back and reflect on my feelings, my needs, and what things I wanted to change.

I captured all of my inner- and outer-world turmoil, but I didn't do much about it. Journaling was my personal pity party. I didn't have the consciousness to use it as fuel for change or transformation. Several years after starting my journals, I remember finding an older journal. I flipped through some of the pages and felt a sharp pain as I realized I was still dealing with some of the big key issues. While I hadn't given up on my desire to transform these things (especially my habit of yo-yo weight gain/loss and my marriage being less than perfect), my lack of progress made me sad.

During those years of living in my head, focusing outward, and DOING, I backed away from consistent Reflection time. I "didn't have time for that kind of stuff." What I know now is that I stubbornly refused to reflect because I was afraid to look that deeply into my life. I sensed that things were out of alignment, and that felt fearful and overwhelming. To avoid these difficult feelings, I shut down emotionally. I carried on with life as usual, going through the motions, mostly living in my head. Family commitments and obligations were my excuse to avoid deep Reflection, except for those few times when I felt at rock bottom in my marriage and my health. I wonder now, if I took a mere ten minutes to ask: "What do I feel? What do I need?"—what would I have learned?

One significant time prior to my awakenings I did mindfully choose to tap in to my Power of Reflection. I had a BIG goal—to win first place in a fitness-related figure competition. I felt a full-body *yes* about that goal. Scared and excited at the same time, I knew I had to step up for myself in a way I had not done in years. I told myself I was willing to do whatever it took to be ready for this competition. I would need to face whatever came up over the twenty-eight weeks leading up to competition in order to succeed. Each day I made time to reflect and journal about my weight-training and cardio workouts, about my mindset, about my food program. I also wrote about my struggles to fully implement what my coach was telling me to do. Voicing my concerns on paper and seeing them as part of my journey to the goal, I became proactive. My intention was to resolve things as quickly as possible, because I had a hard deadline, and any delay would impact my ability to succeed. I felt a big fire under me.

One particular struggle was to have all the food available that I was supposed to eat. That may sound trivial for people who love to cook, but I rarely enjoyed cooking. So, this was a challenge. Although I had been given a meal plan, I scrambled to have everything available when I needed to eat it. My journal Reflections revealed several things: (1) I was going to the grocery store several times a week; (2) I was cooking every day, sometimes multiple times; (3) I wasn't always eating on time, because sometimes I was away from home. How I showed up around food would not work for the duration of the training, and that created a lot of inner tension. I shared my insights and struggles with my trainer, and that evoked an empowering conversation that inspired me to block out time weekly to cook and pre-portion several days' worth of food at a time. What a difference that made! These two changes saved me a ton of time and effort, and soon my concerns and frustration were gone. No major drama, no giving up on my dream. Reflection and action got me back on track. Reflection helped and continues to help me course correct and to pivot when necessary.

I continued the process for every situation that led up to competition day. Reflection kept me moving forward, and I handled each obstacle with more grace and ease. Not only was I fully prepared physically, I was also emotionally stronger for having faced issue after issue. Reflection would serve me well when my awakenings started to occur, starting with my cancer diagnosis.

When I received the cancer diagnosis, I made a conscious habit to spend time in Reflection. Not just to journal, but also to listen. I listened and meditated along with my journaling time. What I wrote in my journal reflected my meditation and listening. I took deeper dives into my life and reflected not only on my health, but also on my relationships, my dreams, and my fears. I left no part of my life unturned. In time, I acknowledged to myself my courage to pursue alternative cancer treatments. I celebrated my decision to speak up to the doctors that rushing into surgery didn't feel right. My journal Reflections indicated I was becoming more vocal about what I needed and what was important to me. As I grew and transformed, I felt pride about the woman I was becoming with every new insight. I was a woman who took a stand and used her voice to express what was important to her.

Reflection has ever since been a cornerstone in my life. I reflect daily, usually multiple times. With this strong habit, I have gracefully navigated a successful divorce mediation, brought to life a heart-centered, inspirational product that started out as a drawing on a paper towel, and deepened my communication with my children. There is power in the noticing and acknowledging! I see in my own life the doors I have opened, the walls I have torn down, and the Radiance I now emit from this beautiful inner work.

Engaging the Power of Reflection expands gratitude and inner peace in minutes.

To strengthen your Power of Reflection, you must understand the magnitude of its power. The Power of Reflection is like rocket fuel that takes you into realms you never knew existed! Reframe your view of the Power of Reflection. Value Reflection as much as the doing, and you will experience profound shifts in your life! Everything you need is at your fingertips—connection to your intuition, to your inner wisdom, and to your higher self. You access these parts of yourself through Reflection. It only takes minutes a day; no need to sit in Reflection all day to experience the benefit. Following are several effective ways strengthen your Power of Reflection.

1. **Add Reflection time into your schedule at the beginning or end of your day (or both).** Reflection will be an easy

habit if you anchor Reflection time in the early or late part of your day. Make sure you have a journal and a pen and find a quiet and comfortable place where you can sit uninterrupted. Set a timer, if needed. Start with ten minutes. Begin by taking a few deep breaths. Clear your mind of any tasks, actions, anxieties, or beliefs in your conscious awareness. Start your timer and listen for what comes up from within. Write it down, and then take another deep breath and listen again. Don't judge or evaluate what comes up during your Reflection time. Simply capture it. Go back later and see what you wrote. Did you learn something new? Do you see a recurring habit, thought, or belief that is holding you back? Did you hear something that brought you joy or happiness? Use this as information about how your life is going or not going.

2. **Direct your focus during Reflection.** Focus on specific areas of your life (self, career, relationships, spirituality, home, recreation, finances) or a specific issue you are experiencing (procrastination, fear, anxiety, loneliness):

   - Begin by taking a few deep breaths to ground yourself.
   - Get into inquiry mode by asking yourself about the area you'd like to reflect on. If it's your business, start by asking: What's new and good? What accomplishments will you acknowledge yourself for? What have you done well? Write whatever comes up for you. Ramp up the power by acknowledging yourself out loud!
   - When you are complete with the celebration, repeat the process for any synchronicities you noticed that day. Recognize what magic was part of your day.
   - Next, ponder what didn't go so well. What did you not do, or what blocks did you face? Write whatever pops up, and then move to inquiry: What might you do to overcome this block in the future? What can you put in

place that will allow you to eliminate this block? Write that down and give yourself a time to do the work.

- Finally, look at your skills and who you are being. What do you see and sense is your next step to grow into the fullest expression of you? What do you need to do with more presence and understanding? Is there something you need to stop doing? Write anything that perks to the surface, and then reflect on one small step that will move you toward being that full version of you.

3. **Once a day, ask *What are you feeling? What do you need?***
   - Begin with a few deep breaths to ground yourself.
   - Ask, "What are you feeling?" Pause to listen for the answer from your inner wisdom (your body, your intuition, or higher self). Simply acknowledge what emerges by repeating, "I see that you are feeling _____." Repeat this process two more times, each time acknowledging what comes up. Validate what you are feeling without judgment or trying to fix things.
   - When you have completed all three rounds of the first question, ask, "What do you need?" Again, listen. If nothing comes up, ask the question again and patiently listen. You might hear a word or phrase, see an image, or feel something in your body. Trust it.
   - The more you ask these two questions, the stronger your listening muscle will be. Write down what comes up for you, and then feel into each item to see if any Inspired Action occurs to you.

A Pause for Reflection: Understanding Your
Embodiment of the POWER OF REFLECTION

In this reflection, you will explore your own experience and embodiment of your Power of Reflection. Grab your journal. Find a quiet place to sit and listen without interruption. Take a couple of deep breaths to get centered and to connect with your inner wisdom. When you are ready, write your responses to the following questions:

1. *In what ways do I see the Power of Reflection in action in my life?*

2. *In what ways have I been limiting or ignoring my connection to the Power of Reflection?*

3. *What next steps can I take to more consciously use my Power of Reflection?*

BONUS MATERIAL

Enter "800011" in the Radiant Achiever APP TRACK NOW page to unlock additional content related to this chapter.

CHAPTER 9

The Power of Ritual

The Power of Ritual has expanded beyond
longstanding cultural traditions.

What comes to mind when you think of ritual? Perhaps you imagine an elaborate ceremony based on hundreds or thousands of years of tradition. Or maybe you visualize a sacred and reverent event that marks a major transition in life, such as a ritual to welcome youth to adulthood, to celebrate a marital union, or to honor the life of someone who has passed away. We see these and hundreds more rituals in cultures across the world. They are the historical or cultural rituals we have learned about and honored through our education, family, and society. Rituals connect people with their heritage. Rituals shape cultures and impact history. Rituals are part of who we are.

In recent times, rituals have expanded into a broader definition and use. We can each create and experience the Power of Ritual in ways that are meaningful for us. Look at current books, make-up brands, clothing, meditation centers, and yoga studios, and you recognize the use of rituals in a mainstream way. At the time of writing this, the beauty brand Rituals (https://www.rituals.com/en-us/about-rituals.html) had a wonderful description and mission that shared a simple definition: "Rituals helps you slow down, and to find happiness in the smallest of things. It is our passion to turn everyday routines into more meaningful rituals." I say *yes* to that. They have since changed the words of their mission, but the sentiment is the same – rituals can take every day moments and elevate them to something deeper and more meaningful.

The Power of Ritual was instrumental not only in my life, but also in my business. The Power of Ritual is a cornerstone element in each of my Mantra Mindset Moments products. Our core message is for women to transform their beauty routine into an uplifting, self-love Ritual. With each purchase, we include a card with a five-step Mindful Moment Radiance Ritual. See the Resources section of this book for more information. By the end of this chapter you will come to understand a new definition of *ritual* that brings sacredness, joy, and peace to your life.

Rituals support you to live consciously and mindfully.

In the context of Radiant Achievement, the Power of Ritual refers to any mindful practice that empowers and uplifts you in some way. Your Rituals can be simple actions or complex ceremonies, based on your personal preferences, experiences, and desires. The daily action of reciting a morning prayer, drinking a cup of coffee or tea, meditating, and sitting in nature are practices many people enjoy daily. What shifts these practices from habits to Rituals is that they are done with mindful presence.

Mindfulness, presence, and consciousness elevate habit to Rituals. Rather than acting on autopilot like most of us do when we brush our teeth, we are very … present … and … aware … during … each … moment of the practice. Yoga instructors remind us to stay present, in the now of each pose and each breath. That is Ritual. Where in your life do you consciously focus on the present and enjoy each breath in each beautiful moment? Maybe yoga, coffee, and tea aren't your thing, but you love being out in nature. Observing the ebb and flow of the ocean, the movement of tree branches in the breeze, or the way the sun's rays bounce off your face—these are all ritualistic practices. You can easily transform any moment of your day into a Ritual.

One benefit of the Power of Ritual is an expanded sense of inner peace.

Rituals help you access all your other Powers of Radiant Achievement. You can create Rituals around each power to enhance and expand them in your experience. For example, to further embody and expand your Power of Authentic Self-Worth, make a daily Ritual of saying (or writing) something you love and appreciate about you. It becomes a Ritual when you not only say the words with mindful presence, but you connect with your body and FEEL the appreciation for yourself. To expand your integration of the Power of Inner Listening, implement a daily ten-minute Ritual of mindful listening; quietly sit and ask your higher self (that all-knowing, intuitive part of you) what it most wants you to know right now. Stay fully present and aware, and you will easily receive the intuitive message.

As you expand your integration and use of the powers, you will come to hear which ones are calling to you for further development. Enhance your hearing of these messages by asking how to enhance the power in your life. Ask what type of daily Ritual will support your development of this power. I created the Mindful Moment Radiance Ritual to further build and develop my connection to my self-worth, although I didn't realize it at the time. I also established a daily ten-minute practice in the early part of my healing journey to strengthen my Power of Inner Listening. These two very simple Rituals had significant impact on the development of my Powers of Radiant Achievement.

Rituals not only support you in building your Powers of Radiant Achievement, they also help you on the path of change as you journey toward your goal. Change and transformation are inevitable, especially as you work to achieve your soul-centered calling. Create and implement Rituals to provide deep support and empowerment as you bravely step out in new ways, let go of old ways of being, and embrace new beliefs that are necessary to reach your goal. Your Rituals keep you grounded and centered during times of uncertainty and discomfort. I implemented a journaling ritual to mindfully sit and write each day for all the times that I took courageous action. This kept me moving forward, even when I felt uncomfortable and unskilled at what I was doing.

As with all the powers, your Rituals are fluid. They will change and expand over time, because you continue to change and expand. Feel into each Ritual as you perform it. How do you feel in the process? Do you resonate with the action? Do you feel centered or have more peace or deeper appreciation and gratitude? When you no longer feel connected to the Ritual, it is time to let it go and create something new. The Power of Ritual supports you to live consciously and mindfully, deepens your gratitude for life, supports you in processing and releasing stuck emotions, helps you to connect with your higher self and to live your most radiant life.

The Power of Ritual helped me shed old, limiting beliefs and transform into the woman I am today.

Rituals excite me. They are my own private moments, morsels of a secret life few people know about. My Rituals are a delicious buffet of different routines and practices that bring joy, peace, empowerment, pleasure, and gratitude to my life. Some of my Rituals feel indulgent, like my morning coffee Ritual; others, like my Mindful Moment Radiance Ritual, open my heart to the fullness of my beauty and open me to bigger possibilities. I love and appreciate the Power of Ritual in my life now, but it wasn't always this way.

I had very few Rituals in my day-to-day life before my awakenings. I laugh here, because my first Ritual that comes to mind is morning coffee. Just thinking of that first hot cup of coffee while I'm looking out the kitchen window at my ocean view, warm and cozy in my favorite pajamas, makes me smile. My Ritual is more than sitting and drinking coffee. My Ritual is to first mindfully connect with each part of the coffee experience. I taste the nuttiness of the roasted bean. I feel the heat of scalding liquid on my mouth and tongue. I watch the twirling steam slowly rise into the air in my cozy kitchen. I smell the warm, roasted scent of hot vapors entering my sleepy nostrils. I hear the sip, sip, sip of my mouth as I excitedly take in those first drinks of my coffee. What joy I experience in this daily Ritual—pleasure that only I know about. I have no desire to share this with anyone but me, myself, and I.

After a few minutes of this quiet pleasure, I expand my awareness to be in gratitude. I feel gratitude for this new day, for my home, my family, and friends. Then I ponder my dreams from the previous evening, ponder my day ahead, connect with the stillness of the day, and appreciate the quiet time. This is one of my favorite times of the day. This simple Ritual of mindfully experiencing my first cup of coffee starts my day in peace and empowerment. I have nothing to worry about, nothing to rush off and do. I am fully present with my thoughts and memories and open to whatever shows up.

As part of my healing journey after my awakenings, I connected with the Power of Ritual in a way I had never done before. Rituals became my private sanctuary from the pain of the early days after my separation. Walking on the beach was an early Ritual I put in place. The beach offered healing properties, and I listened to my calling to take a solo, mindful walk on a regular basis.

I enjoyed Ritual beach walks weekly to reconnect me to my bigger life vision, to recognize how much more there was to my life than what was happening right now. One early fall afternoon as I drove to the beach, I reminded myself that I had no agenda for my walk except to be present with Mother Ocean. My good-parking karma was at play as I pulled up to my favorite location and got the last spot available. I felt heavy with grief, as if I were wearing a fifty-pound weighted vest. My feet hit the ground with a thud as I simultaneously pulled my heavy heart and body out of the car. Oh, how I needed to connect with the sand and healing waters of the ocean. Oh, how I needed to feel its warmth and to see its expansive glory; I knew what I saw would be a reflection of what is inside me. My mind was numb, and my heart wept. I was unaware of thoughts, but felt heart-tears flowing through my body as I slowly climbed the short set of mossy, wooden stairs to the platform that led to the beach. I felt out of breath from the short climb, but the feeling went away when I lifted my gaze from the stairs. I got my first glimpse of joy. Mother Ocean welcomed me with her mesmerizing voice. Each lap, lap, lap of her glistening waves beckoned me to come closer and spend time in her healing power. In a burst of energy, I scurried down the other side of the platform: one, two, three, four, five, six, SAND. My heart burst with joy, and a tear puddled in the corner of my right eye. I felt like I had just arrived home after a long trip away from my family. Love surrounded me as I took off my flip-flops and wiggled my tired toes in the warm, gritty, welcoming sand. My grandpa used to playfully rub his whiskers on my cheek when he kissed me hello, and the sand felt the same way and put the same smile in my heart.

Oh, how I love the beach! It is a slice of heaven on earth. I walked her shores that afternoon and cried, stomped, and sat crouched in pain. Mother Ocean compassionately loved me back with everything she had. My tears flowed into her endless pools as she whisked my pain away on the waves receding from the shoreline. I soaked up her beauty and her peace, and I noticed the smallest of shells, seemingly lost among the trillions of grains of sand. I gently held this tiny ocean treasure, careful not to disturb its curves; I took a closer look and another tear welled up in my eye. She was tiny, but she was oh, so beautiful. Her tiny specialness touched my heart. Gratitude welled up in me. I realized I might have missed her if I hadn't been present to the beauty around me. How often I had missed the beauty in myself and others?

I gently put the shell back in the sand and looked up to see the sun beginning her descent behind the clouds and the horizon. She showed me her Radiance as she took her sweet time to step down until she was fully behind the horizon. I shifted from lightness to feeling energized as I realized the sun's Radiance was a reflection of the Radiance inside of me. Thank you, Mother Sun; thank you Mother Ocean. I no longer felt heavy. My heart shed no more tears.

My weekly beach Ritual cleansed and renewed me. I could see and connect with the beauty and Radiance of nature and ultimately reconnect with these hidden parts of myself. My Rituals were sacred and powerful moments that guided me on my path of mindfulness and inner healing.

My daily routine of the Mindful Moment Radiance Ritual ignited something in me that could not be snuffed out.

A most transformative Ritual that I still do today is mirror work. I incorporate it with the Mindful Moment Radiance Ritual using the Mantra Makeup Mat™. When I created it, I had no idea it would plunge me into a depth of self-love and commitment to my dreams that I hadn't felt in a very long time. I knew the five-step Mindful Moment Radiance Ritual needed to be something I would do, something I resonated with, something that gave me results. My reflections after my mirror work revealed a pattern—a pattern of connection, acknowledgement, and appreciation. I needed to deepen this Ritual for myself before I could ever teach it to someone else.

I pondered each of my newly created Mantra Makeup Mat™ designs, and one in particular touched my heart. It was the Beauty design with the mantra, "Beauty is being the best version of me, inside and out." My heart pinged when I read the mantra, because I knew that I hadn't been showing up as the best version of me prior to my awakenings. I was ready and craving to do that now, and this is the mantra I took into my morning Radiance Ritual for the next few weeks.

There I was in front of my mirror, ready to perform the Mindful Moment Radiance Ritual. I rolled out my elegant, purple makeup mat on the counter in front of me. Step one of the Ritual was complete. I shifted slightly to the left so my sleepy, unmasked reflection was dead center in the mirror and dutifully performed step two: I took three deep breaths and looked deeply into my eyes. I flashed on a memory of me as a little girl with big brown eyes full of sparkle. I felt a rush of love for the younger version of me and wondered if she was still with me. I greeted myself with a warm, "Hello, Christine," and chose to believe that, indeed, this younger version of me was still here.

I looked deeper into my eyes and spoke out loud, "I am proud of you for never giving up on your dreams." I took a deep breath and let that statement fill every cell in my body. It was true! I was proud of my commitment to stick with things that were important to me. My pride deepened as I renewed my conviction to myself and my dreams. I was ready to tackle the day, to face my fears, to listen to my intuition, to shift my mindset, to do whatever I needed to do and be to achieve my dreams—and I felt a renewed energy to do so.

Day after day, week after week, I held this time sacred to connect with my brilliance. Each time I looked at my reflection in the mirror and stated my mantras and spoke my personal gratitude, a larger piece of my brilliance was revealed. I felt my power, beauty, and courage more and more each time. My secret thought about my greatness expanded within me. I held back nothing in front of the mirror. My reflection had nowhere to go. She was front and center in my life. She could not hide; she could only stand tall and take the praise, compliments, and acknowledgement that I gave her. She surrendered and soaked in each loving word.

My daily Mindful Moment Radiance Ritual ignited a flame in me that could not be stopped. I was done playing small. I was done denying my greatness. This was me, and I was going to see and feel with every fiber of my being what I was about and what I had to offer the world. This two-minute daily Ritual was intensely powerful. I was like a train being loaded with coal, and when my furnace was full, I took off for the long trip. There came a point in my daily

Ritual that I realized there was no turning back; that was me. My Ritual had grounded me, supported me to see what is possible, and was now propelling me toward my future. I didn't know the path, but I was ready to go. I left the station to explore what life and my calling had to offer. That is the Power of Ritual in action.

You can create an unlimited number of Rituals.

Anything you do can become a Ritual if you decide it to be. Typically, anything you do consistently that centers you, connects you with gratitude, connects you with your true essence, or supports you on your journey toward your goal and a fulfilling life can be a Ritual. Below are some Rituals that I use and have used to empower my life. Try them out and see which ones resonate for you. There is no right or wrong here. Performing Rituals is a personal practice, and only you will know which ones support you.

1. **Make the Mindful Moment Radiance Ritual part of your morning routine.** You can download a free copy here: http://www.mantramindsetmoments.com/radiance-ritual/
2. **In your journal, create a gratitude list about you.** Note the qualities, traits, gifts, and talents you love and appreciate about you. Write about at least five things daily. Feel deep gratitude for you as you write each item.
3. **Set a reminder on your phone to pause periodically throughout the day.** Take several mindful deep breaths and feel your breath go in and out.
4. **As you plan your agenda for the day, set an intention to be mindful and totally present for all your tasks.** Block small increments of time for 100% focus.
5. **Listen to your self-talk; pay attention to what you say to YOU.** Reframe your negative self-talk to positive, and acknowledge yourself for making the shift.

6. **Schedule breaks into your day; give yourself space just to BE.** No action or thoughts are required!
7. **Get out in nature and notice your connection to its beauty.** Breathe in everything you see.
8. **Move your body to music; place your attention on what your body feels as you move freely to the music.** Thank your body for supporting you.
9. **Meditate.** Long, short, guided, walking, set to music or a timer, there are so, so, so many ways to meditate. Meditation is a MUST do for anyone to live her most radiantly fulfilling life—a life turned on!

A Pause for Reflection: Understanding Your Embodiment of the POWER OF RITUAL

In this reflection, you will pause to recognize your own experience and embodiment of your Power of Ritual. Grab your journal. Find a quiet place to sit and listen without interruption. Take a couple of deep breaths to get centered and to connect with your inner wisdom. When you are ready, write your responses to the following questions:

1. *In what ways do I see the Power of Ritual in my life?*

2. *In what ways have I been limiting or ignoring my connection to the Power of Ritual?*

3. *What next steps can I take to more consciously engage the Power of Ritual?*

BONUS MATERIAL

Enter "800012" in the Radiant Achiever APP TRACK NOW page to unlock additional content related to this chapter.

PART 3

Becoming Your Most Radiant Self

Answering the call to become your most radiant self is an act of self-love that fuels your journey toward your ever-evolving soul callings.

CHAPTER 10

Being A Radiant Leader

*Owning your power as a Radiant Leader will
bring opportunities to serve and influence in
ways you might never have imagined.*

In the prior chapters, you learned seven core powers that support
you to achieve your goals, dreams, and callings with joy, ease, and
flow, and to allow your innate Radiance to shine. These Powers of
Radiant Achievement not only help you achieve your goals, they also
support you to become and be a RADIANT LEADER.

Radiant Leaders are a new breed who lead under a new paradigm
for leadership. This new breed of leader embodies the Powers of
Radiant Achievement to make a difference in her personal world and
the world at large. Radiant Leaders source their power from inside.
Answering a calling or seeing a vision she desires to bring to life,
a Radiant Leader is deeply connected to WHAT she is doing and
WHY she is doing it. Radiant Leaders engage the Powers of Radiant
Achievement to bring their vision to life. Although I see myself this
way now, I didn't always embrace the role.

My journey to become a Radiant Leader unfolded beautifully.

In my own journey, I transitioned from embodying the Powers
of Radiant Achievement to owning my strengths and ultimately
stepping into BEING a Radiant Leader. We all have small moments
of choice—moments that move us closer to our highest life or keep

us stuck circling the mountain, as I like to say. I clearly remember one such moment when my journey took a positive step forward. It was the day I said *yes* to pursuing my calling to create the Mantra Makeup Mat™.

My inner voice said, "This is what leading looks like. This is what listening to your soul looks like. This is what taking a stand for your fullest life looks like." Saying *yes* that day and following through on my idea created a subtle but significant inner shift. The inner shift was one of responsibility for MY life, a shift that allowed me to let go of the belief that I needed others' approval and that my idea had to make sense before I pursued it. This shift forever blasted that old mountain I had been circling for years and freed me to take initial steps as a Radiant Leader.

Since then, I have used the Powers of Radiant Achievement consciously in my work—to expand my programs, my platform, and my impact. I let go of old stories that kept me from using my voice. I expanded my connection with my worth as a person and as a coach. I experienced breakdowns, breakthroughs, lots of flow, and synchronicities as I achieved my business intentions. Over time, a new confidence grew inside me, a confidence connected to the bigger ME that catapulted me to a new level of Radiant Leadership.

It was the fall of 2018. I was participating in a woman's group program. One particular activity shifted things up for me, leading to a big *aha*. We were asked to list women we admired—someone alive or deceased, someone we personally knew or had heard of, a public or private figure. Our next step was to write the qualities we admired in each one of these women. Easy enough! The final step was to look over the list and see what they all had in common. Each of the women on my list were change makers in some way. The punch line, our facilitator said, was that whatever I discovered was a reflection of who I AM. Wowza! That was a big one to take in. I felt resistant to seeing myself that way.

Our astute instructor then led us through a partner exercise where we recited out loud our newly discovered quality. We were told to feel this quality within ourselves. It wasn't about reciting a statement, it was about saying it with feeling and embodying the quality. I found it difficult to admit and to say out loud, at first. I was embarrassed to make this bold statement about myself, but I knew in my heart it was true.

After several minutes, I GOT IT. I connected with the me who IS a change maker. For the first time ever, I wholeheartedly felt and saw myself as a change maker. Owning that was a pivotal moment when I stepped more fully and courageously onto my path as a Radiant Leader. My turning point further deepened my commitment to listen to and pursue the callings of my soul and to honor my deeper life's purpose.

Are you beginning to see how you are already a Radiant Leader? Are you excited to step more fully into your power as a Radiant Leader? What is one thing you can do right now to BE a Radiant Leader? What is one outcome that owning your abilities as a leader will bring to your life? Your journey as a Radiant Leader will continue to unfold, as mine did, perfectly. Stay open for information, connection, aha moments, and opportunities to be the Radiant Leader you were born to be!

Radiant Leaders are all around you.

In my ongoing journey to expand my influence as a Radiant Leader, I pay close attention to the women I interact with. What are they doing? Who are they being? What qualities do they possess? How do they show up when faced with a challenge? How do they show up when things go well? Radiant Leadership affects every area of life—the small, personal scale (yourself) and the larger scale (your family or community). I have encountered women who exemplify Radiant Leadership at business networking events, in my friend circles, and even at the grocery store.

Some of them have fancy, formal titles; others have no title at all. Young or older, they are all young at heart. They are outspoken, and they are quiet and reflective. They are imperfect, and they are okay with that! They each have a glow about themselves as they do the work they are called to. They all handle their tasks and responsibilities with a grace and ease. They remain centered and grounded despite turmoil around them, and they are not easily rattled by the latest news of the day. They remain steady and steadfast in their purpose, and while they are aware of what is happening around them, they carefully choose what to be involved in or not. They stayed connected to their contribution. If they get off track, they reconnect and re-center, regardless of what others are doing. They don't compare themselves to others; rather, they celebrate others' success.

Following are stories of five amazing Radiant Leaders that I have the pleasure to know and work with who have impacted my life and inspired me to step even more courageously into my leadership, into my role as a change maker, and into my Radiance. I interviewed each about her journey to answer her calling and asked how she used a Power of Radiant Achievement to propel her forward. You can access the full interviews through the links in the Bonus Material in the Radiant Achiever App. Details are at the end of this chapter.

Marsh Engle shares her connection with the Power of Commitment.

My mentor and coach, Marsh Engle, is a Radiant Leader. I first saw her speak at a day-long event where she was the main speaker. Her spunky, five-foot frame exuded energy and enthusiasm. When she spoke, I felt her power and commitment to guide women to become leaders in their lives and their businesses. I immediately wanted to know her better and to explore working with her. I wanted to be MY version of how she showed up and interacted with us that day. I had the joy of digging deep into her own Radiant Achievement and Radiant Leadership for my initial podcast episode! Her responses to two key questions are below:

Christine: Can you remember the moment when you felt a calling to create or develop one of these amazing pieces of work that you're developing? Really take us into that moment in your life when you felt that calling and tell us what that was like for you.

Marsh: Several distinctive times come to mind. One of those times was deciding to leave my business and career to investigate, study and research the lives of Amazing Woman. I wanted to know and understand the inner dimensions of the amazing woman. Even though I had accomplished on a material level what many considered to be important; and I guess at the time, I thought to be significant, too. But over time what I came to see is that there was a wide gap between my values and my actions – I longed to understand my own worth, awaken my spiritual connection. The motivating question that moved me: In a world where feminine qualities are so undervalued, how can I begin to weave my spiritual values into my work?

So, I journeyed out. I called it: 'a search for the Amazing Woman.' I began interviewing women from every walk of life – I was looking to learn where their passions stemmed from, how she found a sense of sovereignty. Where did she find the core of her self-definition? What did she stand for? That led me to meet and speak with some truly amazing women, and I began to write a series of books about them. That was a pivotal, transformational moment for me. That's when I discovered how I could begin to serve others through my work.

I know you talk a lot about our soul-centered calling and I believe that calling happened when my mom died. My mom was very influential in my life, because of the level of love she gave. When she passed, I felt the call to search for the amazing woman. I felt in my heart that she was saying to me, "It's your time. It's your time to discover who you are — the amazing woman within you." That's what prompted me to write the books, interview women, and eventually establish Amazing Woman's Day, which grew into a movement, inspiring and impacting thousands of women's lives.

Amazing Woman's Day ran for ten years. Then, I felt an awakening to move to the next level of my calling. I was sitting on a Maui beach in deep contemplation. I wondered, and I don't mean this to sound morbid, but I wondered, had I already completed the work that I came here to complete? Amazing Woman's Day programs and events had reached into many parts of the world and had touched many, many lives. The movement itself had a life of its own – women within the movement had elevated their leadership, messages and work. They were doing work and leading communities touching and impacting thousands of lives. The Amazing Woman movement was well on its' way to transforming the culture of women's success and leadership.

I wondered: Have I completed the work I came here to achieve? Is my legacy complete? And the answer I heard was a resounding NO – followed by the words: "a call to lead". What I found is that as we step more fully into our purpose, we evolve. And, as we evolve, we create the space for our calling to expand — take on a new definition. But that requires we fully commit to elevating our self-image – and step more fully into how we define our capacity to serve.

For me that expanded capacity to serve took shape as establishing the Amazing Woman Nation. I felt moved to create social impact programs – campaigns, books and products that would bring women together so we can collectively invest our voices, rise in our feminine power, transform the world. I believe collaboration, collectively working together in community, dynamically elevates our capacity to serve. We are so much more together than we are isolated and alone.

Christine: What has that Power of Commitment meant to you and your journey to pursue your callings?

Marsh: The commitment piece is so important, it's vital. At some level commitment has been a driving force in the lives and work of every amazing woman I've interviewed and worked with. It's the distinguishing factor. As we consider what it takes to commit we can quickly see that it relates to anchoring in—anchoring into all you are willing to take a stand for, be and create. What are you willing to stand for? What do you see missing in the world?

Back in 1999, when I first stepped out into what I now know to be my calling, I was moved to understand the true power of feminine leadership and success – what needed to happen for women to awaken the fullness of her feminine power in every area of her life. And I was willing to take a stand for it, make a wholehearted commitment to lead the march into a more balanced, embodied, integrative approach to work and life. That began with my own willingness to do the same.

Commitment relates to intention. And it is intention that guides the words we speak, the decisions we make, the actions we take – how we invest our creative vision. When we're committed and anchor into what we know we stand for – what we are willing to stand for – we are much more likely to stand strong, inspired, deliberate and impactful.

When the Amazing Woman movement launched, and I took a committed stand to feminine success and leadership, I didn't fully understand where it would take me. But I was willing to commit to knowing. I was willing to commit to learning. I was willing to commit to discovering. Early in the movement, my commitment was a statement of: I am willing to discover. Then my commitment grew into: I'm willing to speak about it – find a way to communicate what I'm discovering and seeing as expanded possibilities. In the beginning that was scary. I had not spoken in front of the camera or behind the mic. But something happened as I stayed true to my commitment — my commitment naturally evolved into: I am willing to serve. It was with this commitment – the commitment to serve – that the truest sense of purpose emerged – the opportunity to wholeheartedly be a part of something bigger – something that is collectively impacting the legacy of women's success and leadership.

The only person that really matters is you validating yourself. I didn't even understand what feminine leadership was. But I was willing to commit to knowing. I was willing to commit to learning. I was willing to commit to discovering it. And so that commitment said, I don't know what this is, but I'm willing to discover it. The next level of commitment might be I don't know how to speak this, but I'm willing to find a way to communicate it. The next level of commitment might be I've never spoken on stages, and I might be a little wobbly, but I'm going to go for it and learn. I'm going to learn from that opportunity to speak about it. I've never been in broadcast media, but I'm going to get in front of the camera or I'm going to get behind the mic and I'm going to experience and I'm going to allow myself to find the commitment of confidence. Commitment to me is a deep relationship. It's a very intimate relationship with one's creativity and one's self-belief.

Sandra Dee Robinson went from self-doubt to self-love. Her journey helped others gain confidence to genuinely share their message.

When I first met Sandra Dee, she was facilitating a class called "Charisma on Camera." I had read her bio prior to the class, so I knew she had spent years on TV as a successful actor. Her professional credentials were outstanding, and I soon realized how lucky I was to be learning from her. Before class even started, she made herself available to say hello and get to know us a bit. Despite my nervousness about meeting a TV star, I felt as if I had known her for years. I felt welcomed by her. Talk about seeing and feeling someone's Radiance—Sandra Dee's genuine smile lit up the room that day! Every time she spoke, she emanated an authentic sense of care for us. It was palpable. She is down to earth, and in her coaching and free online groups she generously shares her knowledge, expertise, and wisdom from her years in front of the camera. Sandra Dee knows about Radiance, and I was honored and excited to interview her on the topic of Radiant Achievement and answering her calling. Here is an excerpt from our interview:

> **Christine: Take me back to that place where you first felt that calling. And it could be about some of your recent work. It could be way back when and how that felt for you and how it unfolded.**

> *Sandra Dee: I had two. Because my first calling, if you want to call it that, and my main calling are actually two. To empower people and help women to realize, see themselves more like God sees them, so that they can move from where they are to where God wants them to be. And I know that that's bringing in the higher power and all that, and if you don't believe in that, then maybe you don't get that. But that's kind of how I feel. And I'm just a facilitator for that.*

> *Whether I'm working with horses, whether I'm working directly with somebody or with a group or a company, it's kind of all the same thing. It's getting people to understand how perfect they are in their own design, that there's nothing wrong with them. In fact, they already have everything that they need in order to get done what is in their heart to do—and to think big and not be afraid to go there and trust that they've got it. You know, I didn't do that.*

> *My first calling was to be a teacher. If you had told me that my calling was going to be that when I was younger, I probably would have crawled under a rock and died, because I could not, I mean, I had school.*

You do those tests to tell you what your skills are good for when you grow up to be a great whatever, and they're a pretty good test. Because when I was little, they said you'd be great teacher. I was so shy, no self-esteem.

If anybody had heard me speak, they might know my story that my closest sibling is fourteen years older than I am. Mom wasn't too crazy about siblings, about children in general, so I'm surprised I have two siblings. But when I came along, I was called the bonus baby.

Mom would rather have the cash back. She was not crazy about me being around. She literally said, "Life would be better if you hadn't been born." That sets the bar a little low for self-esteem when you're a young girl. So, my first calling was to find a way to survive that and get away from that. But I didn't know what I was doing. I got introduced to acting when I was in school, and I thought how fun. I can be someone else, because I'm not worthy of being here. And when I become someone else, I had people telling me good things. That was acceptance, which I wasn't getting from my mother. You can see how that was a survival mechanism that was for me get to the next thing. I became successful in that, and I was making a lot of money and I had this platform. And as you said, I've always been drawn to animal causes or whatever people might identify with, whatever their charity, whatever their heart is set on, whatever problem in the world they would like to solve. My heart was in that.

I had this platform, and I liked to work with women and show them they have a platform wherever they are. You don't have to be an actor to have a platform.

If you don't think you have one, we can create one for you. But I had TV, always being interviewed, and I was afraid to look people in the eye. I wasn't good to fans in the beginning, because I thought, "Why would they want to talk to me?" Completely a disconnect between the girl walking down the red carpet and the girl who wouldn't walk into a room where she didn't know anybody. That was a real problem. And that's where the second calling started to come forth, which was having to figure out who the heck I was.

Why was I even here? I was humiliated at an audition once, because it was for an infomercial. We used to call it hush money, because you can make a lot of money doing infomercials. I was on TV every day doing my soap, and so, they thought, "Oh, she's going to be great." So, I came in to audition, and the casting director said, "Just be yourself." Right. Anyone who has been on video with a videographer who says, "Oh, just be yourself," when you don't have anything in that file—that sets you flailing. I mean tell me to be Mrs. Santa Clause. Tell me to be a peach. Tell me, tree. Right. But tell me to be myself—what, are you crazy? That's not worthy of being. And so, I set off hiring performance coaches, because I failed that day. I left in tears. He looked like he was disappointed. I was pitiful, and it was humiliating, and I cried for the two-hour ride home. I was in L.A. and I was only going six miles, but it's two hours on the freeway. Yeah, you know that.

So that was the moment of change. I hired performance coaches, and I learned that performance is not where I needed to change. I needed to change from the inside. And that was sometimes a difficult journey. Yes, some resistance there. But as I started to peel away the layers of that protection around my heart and around everything, I realized something: I am designed to be a teacher. I actually am that. And it's not because I'm better than everybody else; it's because I know how it is to not feel so great about yourself. I know how it is to feel like you're failing at reaching your potential and maybe not even knowing what your potential is. So that's what.

And now I work with brilliant people, but at every level of success there is something that will undermine your confidence. It could be something your mother said to you, even though you're making a million bucks a year; something that comes up and haunts you at just the wrong time. And you're like, I thought I got rid of that. When people say what kind of coach are you, I'm a communication and business coach. Because communication starts with the relationship you have with yourself. Then there's your videos, your speaking, and all of that is the communication, the relationship you have with your market. But it starts with you.

Christine: *Right, right. So, what I love, what really struck me when you were talking is this core of the teacher, the supporter, the coach. To help people understand and love and appreciate their brilliance; it's foundational to who you are. And then that outlet, the expression of it, is what's been changing over time. Right? So, you went through your work and figured that out for yourself. And now you're kind of going back to your roots. The early test said, you're a teacher, although you had no connection back then. But now you can see it.*

Sandra Dee: *Yeah. So, I think we have callings to maybe get our first job. You know, we feel like we found our calling. I thought my calling was to go be an actor. And then once I fixed the broken part of me who needed the acting in order to survive, I started asking. I didn't need it anymore. I didn't need to be quiet anymore, and so I said what can I do? And somebody said, "Help women." This was my first. Help women make videos for their business. Okay, so that's what launched Charisma on Camera all those years ago, and it's just sort of morphed because I fell in love with my clients. And I worked to get them comfortable on camera by helping them find out who they are.*

Unless you find out who you are, and you're given that freedom of expression, you don't market with your core nature. But not being somebody else, not acting as if, just being who you are and living, as you said, radiating, all the brightness that is within you. Then, if you're authentic with that, you attract the people you really want to have into your business, to work alongside of you, to be your clients and your customers. And that's when life feels abundant. It's even more to me than making sure somebody makes money. I say that I help people increase their sales and revenue, but it's really about helping them create that life of abundance. Usually that includes building up your sales and your revenue.

Christine: One of the Powers of Radiant Achievement is Authentic Self-Worth. I'd love to hear from you, how has owning your Authentic Self-Worth supported you in your journey of life and pursuing your callings?

Sandra Dee: *I think there's so much richness there. And I say that with complete gratitude that there's so much richness there. Because richness is not in your bank account. I had that, but I didn't have self-worth. That is not a life of abundance. But once I started to appreciate who I am, I realized that I was believing things that weren't true and that I did have a lot of potential. Even now, I feel like I have potential hopefully when I'm eighty. I hope it keeps going, because at every turn in life I think we're gifted something that we can share. I hope that continues for me as long as possible.*

But I think that the biggest gift of self-worth is that once I own mine, I am able to bring it out in others. If I didn't own mine, it's like that stupid thing that everybody says about being on the airplane. I can't believe I'm mentioning this, it's so cliché. But the whole mask thing, okay. It's the same way with owning that relationship with yourself—it has to come first, and then you can work on healing other people. You can share that love with other people. And I did not feel very loving until I learned to do that. I would never have been able to build the business that I built, to be able to see potential in others. Today I had several phone calls that just lit me up because of the potential of people that I'd be able to reach and give them that encouragement.

I think owning the authentic worth is vital. Honestly, I never would have been able to land my husband until I recognized what I was worth or at least started to recognize what I was worth. I've grown a lot since I've been with him, which is a blessing, since he's the guy to bring that out of me. But until I did that, I was dating all the wrong guys. I wasn't dating guys who had potential. That story's a whole other podcast. That's just some of the little nuggets that came from that work on my self-worth.

Janice Kameir, a corporate gal with a deep, spiritual life, could no longer deny her natural gift of mediumship.

I consider numerous close friends as "soul sisters." Each one of my soul sisters believes she is first a spiritual being and second a human being. Janice Kameir is no exception. We have shared deep conversations about our spiritual life—our beliefs, connection with our angels, love we feel from God, surrendering to our higher purpose, and related topics that moved us to lean in as we shared, reflected, and on many occasions laughed! As Janice was a highly-successful corporate HR executive, I was intrigued when our conversations moved toward her acceptance and development of her gift as a spiritual medium. For years, she had tried to deny this calling. She was a corporate gal; how could this be her? Her story will brighten your day. Her responses to two key questions follow:

Christine: I want to talk specifically about you feeling the calling regarding mediumship and how you stepped into that. Can you remember that moment when you felt called to be a medium or how that all transpired and unfolded for you?

Janice: About eight years ago, I was driving home from work and I thought, I don't know if I can do corporate America too much longer. I've had a great career. I've been blessed, and at the same time it felt like something was missing. I remember thinking, how could I explore my passions? What are my passions? It was an inner, soulful discussion.

I thought, I really love to learn. I'm curious, I want to learn. So, the first step I decided, was to enroll into a motivational seminar or a weekend retreat somewhere. Just see what that looks like. The retreat I chose was more of a spiritual retreat, and I wasn't sure what I was getting into. I was open minded going into it. The entire weekend I was on a high. I knew I had connected with my passion, just within that workshop. I didn't know then that I would be a medium. That was something that came up later, but I knew that my purpose was somewhere in the area of spirituality as a result of that weekend retreat.

Out of that I also realized that I wanted to connect people more with their loved ones, with God as a whole, understanding the spiritual realm and the angelic realm. That's about all I knew at that time. Maybe a year later one of my deceased loved ones came into me. I had heard that other people have had this experience. I was not a doubter, I just hadn't experienced it before, so I didn't know what to think. From there I started studying mediumship, because I now had this experience behind me. I've been working with mentors for the last few years to help me develop my gifts. I have had the good fortune of channeling the souls of loved ones for more than six years now.

Christine: I'd like to dive a little bit into your Inner Listening. And you mentioned meditation. Tell us how you have developed that muscle of Inner Listening and what you do on a daily or ongoing basis.

Janice: I did a lot of meditation, which I did bring into corporate America. I do guided meditation twice a week. That's two full hours of meditation, which is great. I also meditate in the morning, right when I get up. If you can carve out five or ten minutes of your time, right when you awake and before your feet hit the ground, you can begin to develop that muscle of Inner Listening. There's a space there, that you can grab a hold of, which is quiet time. That is where the listening occurs. It's hard to find quiet time throughout our days so that helps me. I also pray on the way to work and I take deep breaths. My newest practice is every time I hit a stop light, I take a deep breath. Then I'm opening up myself more to the Universe, which is another way of receiving. And I've also done sugar cleanses. The more I clean and keep my body cleansed, the more I'm going to receive. It's a mind-body connection.

Rebecca Casciano's passion for beauty and her personal struggle with a health issue tilled the perfect soil for her calling to emerge.

I connected with this next amazing Radiant Leader through the power of social media. I scrolled through Facebook and Instagram, and (as happens) one thing lead to another. I was researching inner beauty, Radiance, and self-love when I stumbled onto Rebecca's account. I learned about her work as a clean beauty makeup artist and her Sacred Beauty Movement and instantly became a fan. Diving into our interview and hearing her story of passion for helping women revealed her to be a Radiant Leader set to make an impact on every woman who crosses her path. Here are her responses to two key questions:

Christine: You've answered, I believe, more than one calling in your life. Share with us when you were feeling that calling, sensing into it, heard it—however it hit you. And then what transpired and unfolded from there as you stepped into pursuing that calling?

Rebecca: *Yes, that's true Christine. I'd love to share. I've been an artist since I was a child, I loved drawing and painting especially. As I got older I'd say my initial calling was to be a working artist of some kind. In high school I studied Advertising Design and then moved to New York City to attend the Fashion Institute of Technology with the goal of being an art director or graphic designer. I soon realized that I didn't enjoy designing on computers, but I wasn't sure what I wanted to do. After some soul searching, experimenting and encouragement from friends, I realized that I wanted to become a makeup artist in the summer of 2000.*

It was interesting because at the same time, I was also struggling with chronic cystic acne, which is the most severe form of acne that you can have. This put me on a life-changing wellness journey that made the connection between inner and outer beauty. I gradually transitioned to a plant-based diet and holistic healing modalities. These lifestyle changes not only helped me heal my skin, but transformed my entire life to one that was more aligned with nature, spirituality and overall wellness.

At times I felt like I was living in two worlds, being a makeup artist and working very much on the outside, but also being connected to spirituality and wellness. I was going along with having these two different worlds, my personal and professional lives until around 2008, when the economy shifted. I wasn't working much and began to ask myself, "What's next? What else am I passionate about?"

What came to me was my passion for wellness and a plant-based lifestyle. I knew what a big impact it had on my own life and approach to beauty. I started to do some research on The Institute for Integrative Nutrition and it was almost instantly that I realized my calling was to help and empower women to embrace their beauty from the inside out. Becoming a health coach allowed me to bring together all of the tools, products and practices that had benefited me so much on my journey.

Christine: What role does the Power of Inspired Action have in your life and in your journey of your movement or living your calling?

Rebecca: Inspired Action is my guiding principle of each day! Over time, I've learned that you can't wait for inspiration, you have to create it. And when you feel inspired, you have to take action, despite any fear. And this is how I felt when I started The Sacred Beauty Movement in 2015. I knew that I loved holding space for women, especially in groups. I knew that inner and outer beauty are so deeply connected, and I want to share this knowledge. I think Inspired Action is about moving forward with intention, even when you don't know where it will lead you.

Thankfully, The Sacred Beauty Movement is still evolving and growing. I currently offer one-on-one Sacred Beauty Coaching and The Sacred Beauty Collective, a virtual community for women to explore inner and outer beauty through self-love, sisterhood and spirituality. Helping women love themselves more, and thus change the world for the better, inspires me to continue on this journey and calling.

Stacy McCarthy lives the Power of Ritual every day.

One day I paused to read a postcard that hung on the community board in my favorite healthy, fast-food restaurant, Beaming. This postcard announced an upcoming workshop called "A Day of Namaste." I loved the design of the postcard (I pay attention to those things), but I also loved the focus of Stacy McCarthy's Day of Namaste message—how we eat, how we think, and how we move. I wanted to meet this Radiant Leader, and I wanted to be part of her event as a participant and vendor. Talking with her gave me additional insights and respect for her clarity of purpose and values. Her responses to two key questions follow:

Christine: I know you've had a long career. Connect us to one of those moments when you felt called to create, to develop, to pursue something that really spoke to you. How did it feel and how did you then pursue this journey?

Stacy: I was fortunate at a young age to really realize what my talents were and what my love was and be able to put that together. I know a lot of people graduate from college and never use their degrees, but I graduated with a degree that I've been able to use throughout my life. I realized that I love movement.

I love personal development. I love wellness. I love people. So, I ended up in exercise physiology, and I had a great career out of college. I worked my way up through a chain of health clubs from an "aerobics instructor" that's what we were called back in the day to COO - Chief Operating Officer.

I was sitting in my office one day, putting out email fires and managing teams throughout the clubs. And I thought this is not what I am supposed to do. While driving home from work that day, I remember the moment that my shoulders dropped away from my ears and I said to myself, "I'm going to resign tomorrow." I resigned because I wasn't doing what I was passionate about. I wanted to be of service at something I had developed a talent for and gave me a sense of contribution.

The CEO was shocked. I had the stock options. I had the paycheck. I had the office with a view. And I said, "It's not fulfilling me." I was in a rigid schedule, and that's not my personality, either. I had young children at home, and I wanted to be more available to them. I wanted to be the master of my schedule. What helped me was identifying my calling, developing my talents and being crystal clear on my values. And when you understand your values clearly, you move towards your calling in a more sustainable way. I had this thing in my head that said, if I screw up my kids, nothing else matters.

So, I rearranged everything, and I started a little home business of teaching yoga and meditation. It was a risk because it was the 1990's and body, mind, spirit wellness was not as prevalent as today. It started slow, finances were drastically reduced from the C-Suite position, but I'd never been happier. Over the decades my career has grown into more than I dreamed of at the time. If I reflect on the three things that gave me direction and the courage to make a change it would be, develop your talents around what you love, discover how that can be of service to others and get clear on your values of what makes you tick.

Christine: I'd love for you to talk about the Power of Ritual. What has Ritual meant to your journey of pursuing your calling?

Stacy: *Everyone already has rituals. Some people have rituals to have a cup of coffee with a donut every morning, but at the end of the day, did it make their life better? What I help people do is develop Super Rituals. If your rituals are directed the right way, they can expand your life in amazing ways. If your rituals are mis-directed, they will lead you to a place that was not consciously designed by you. Some people don't want a disciplined life. But for me, a disciplined life makes me sleep better, makes me function better, and still lets me feel the whimsy and the joy and the fun of doing things. Rituals give me consistency, and the discipline brings me an inner peace.*

And so, my teaching is about creating these lifelong Super Rituals and mastering what I call the Big Three: how you move, how you eat, and how you think, all wrapped up in namaste. And for those who are like, "What is namaste?" and they're not into yoga, namaste is a Sanskrit word that means, essentially, the divine light in me bows, honors, and sees the divine light in you. When you are in that place and I am in that place, we are one.

It's about seeing the oneness and the pure love. When I eat well, I have rituals for eating. When I move intelligently and mindfully, I have rituals for that, and when I work on strengthening my mind, I have rituals for that. And you wrap it up in the component of love, of seeing it within yourself and in everyone you connect with. The Super Rituals that go along with that are the rituals that I teach. If you do these Super Rituals, I believe that you will have more joy in your life physically, mentally, emotionally, and spiritually, and probably financially, as well.

Please watch or listen to the full interviews in the Radiant Achiever App (under TOPICS). We dive deep into questions related to unexpected turns in their journey, new personal powers they discovered, and their own definitions of Radiant Achievement. I guarantee you will take away huge doses of inspiration and courage from each of these beautiful, radiant souls!

As these examples show, Radiant Leaders are in all walks of life. These women have different backgrounds, different gifts, and different callings. What they all have in common is that they are fulfilling a calling of their soul and are BEING their most radiant self. Be on the lookout for the Radiant Leaders around you. Be present and aware of their qualities and acknowledge where you also have those qualities. Be inspired and influenced by these women to more fully own and step into your Radiant Leadership, which leads me to a special invitation for you.

**I invite you to claim your power and
step into Radiant Leadership.**

This chapter is all about being a Radiant Leader, and I want to make sure you know that you, too, are a Radiant Leader. My special invitation is for you to see yourself and claim your power as a Radiant Leader. Right here, right now, see yourself as a Radiant Leader.

If you already consider yourself a leader in your personal or professional life, congratulations! If you find it difficult or impossible to see yourself as a leader, reading this book is your call to do something different. Some people resist title of *leader*, because they define leadership from a masculine perspective and not from a radiant perspective. Some people think they are too old, too weak, too shy, too poor, too this or that. If that's true for you, please put it aside—it is irrelevant!

What does a Radiant Leader look like? Radiant Leaders tap into their innate powers, the Powers of Radiant Achievement. Using these powers lets you see yourself differently and connect deeply with the fullness of what you are capable of and who you are capable of being. It lets you see how your innate passions are connected with the world at large. It lets you see past your short-term goals. It lets you recognize your unique qualification to positively impact the lives of others. You awaken to see situations where you can put your passions into action. Sensing that full body *yes*, you, as a Radiant Leader, will take inspired action to affect change. You are a reflection of Gandhi's message to become the change you wish to see in the world.

Four key shifts allow you to fully step into your natural capacity to lead.

In my work with other leaders, change makers, and influential women, I have noticed numerous traits that support them to make big impact. These traits are a result of their Radiant Shifts—shifts in how they live and lead in their life. I invite you, dear Radiant Leader, to claim these shifts for yourself. In doing so, you claim both your POWER and IMPACT as a Radiant Leader:

RADIANT SHIFT #1: TAKE RADICAL RESPONSIBILITY FOR YOUR LIFE

When you take responsibility for your life and your results and outcomes, you own your power. When you take full responsibility for everything in your life, not only will you live a vibrant, radiant, and fulfilling life, you will also influence the world. Radical responsibility for your life frees you to own and pursue your desires. Radical responsibility means you don't need permission from anyone other than yourself.

RADIANT SHIFT #2: COMMIT TO FOLLOWING YOUR UNIQUE CALLING

There is no one-size-fits-all when it comes to being a Radiant Leader. Your connection with your inner callings determines the type of leader you will be and how you will bring your callings to the world. You may be called to impact one person, your family, your city, or the world. We each play a unique role, and it is counterproductive to compare ourselves and our contribution with others, men or women.

RADIANT SHIFT #3: COMMIT TO CONTINUED GROWTH AND LEARNING BY STRENGTHENING YOUR POWERS OF RADIANT ACHIEVEMENT

When you commit to apply and strengthen your Powers of Radiant Achievement, you will continue expanding your empowerment and impact. Your lifelong journey will continue to unfold and expand in ways you cannot imagine. In 1986, did Oprah Winfrey know where she'd be today? Do you think she had any idea where her commitment to leadership and to pursue her callings would take her, or that her impact would be so profound? No, and that's the secret. You will have no idea; what a terrific effect of Radiant Leadership that is! Focus on answering your current calling and apply the Powers of Radiant Achievement. When you achieve your calling (or possibly even before), you will hear the murmurings of your next calling. Beautiful things unfold when you say *yes* to you!

RADIANT SHIFT #4: CONNECT WITH OTHER RADIANT LEADERS

One final step to expand your power as a Radiant Leader is to join and stay connected with a community of other Radiant Leaders. Support is critical to pursue living your fullest life. It may feel scary to share your new dreams and visions with people who have only seen you in one way. I experienced that, myself. Find a community you resonate with, whether it is one other person, a small group, or a global community. Connect on a regular basis to celebrate your successes, to give and receive support and reflections about your struggle points, and to be encouraged no matter what perceived obstacle you face. Community connection is a path for leadership. Your journey, insights, and goals will inspire others to their highest potentials. I invite you to join the community of Radiant Leaders on my private Facebook group: http://www.facebook.com/groups/theRadiantAchievementInnerCircle

Give yourself (and the world!) a precious gift: Tap into and strengthening your power as a Radiant Leader. You carry inside you all the seeds of Radiant Leadership! It's part of your coding, your DNA. You can lead without having a formal leadership title. You are a leader, regardless of titles. Engage your leadership by claiming your power and using it in your unique way, whether to lead yourself through your daily routines, to lead your family, or to lead a cultural revolution that affects the world.

A Pause for Reflection: Understanding Your
Embodiment as a Radiant Leader

In this reflection, you will look at your own experience and embodiment as a Radiant Leader. Grab your journal. Find a quiet place to sit and listen without interruption. Take a couple of deep breaths to get centered and to connect with your inner wisdom. When you are ready, write your responses to the following questions:

1. *In what ways do I define and value myself as a Radiant Leader?*

2. *In what ways have I been limiting or giving away my power as a Radiant Leader?*

3. *What next steps can I take to more consciously step into and expand my ability to be a Radiant Leader?*

BONUS MATERIAL

Enter "800013" in the Radiant Achiever APP TRACK NOW page to unlock additional content related to this chapter.

CHAPTER 11

Living A Radiant Lifestyle

*When you live a Radiant Lifestyle, Radiance
becomes you, in everything you do.*

You can apply the Powers of Radiant Achievement to every aspect of
your life and set yourself up to live a Radiant Lifestyle! You probably
have a vision for what you desire in your career, health, finances,
relationships, spirituality, home environment, and recreation. Your
LIFE—your days, weeks, and months—are full of moment-by-
moment decisions that either support your vision or not. To continue
moving toward your highest visions every day, use the Powers of
Radiant Achievement in day-to-day decision making. That is how
to live a Radiant Lifestyle.

A Radiant Lifestyle is lived from the inside out, embodying the
Powers of Radiant Achievement, as the fullest expression of you
unfolds. Living a Radiant Lifestyle is less about *yes* or *no,* but more
about degrees. A Radiant Lifestyle can be dimmed or brightened,
just like a beautiful chandelier with a dimmer switch. Your lifestyle
will be more radiant the more you embody and strengthen your
Powers of Radiant Achievement—Authentic Self-Worth, Mindset,
Inner Listening, Inspired Action, Commitment, Reflection, and
Ritual.

In your Radiant Lifestyle, you are consciously connected to your
inner self. You love and accept yourself for where you are now, and
at the same time, compassionately work to shed limiting beliefs and

stories, so that you can pursue your callings and live your fullest life. Being on the journey is living a Radiant Lifestyle, a fluid expression of your essence, from the goals you pursue to the leadership roles you take on, and especially in who you are BEING. When you live a Radiant Lifestyle, Radiance becomes you, in everything you do!

Living a Radiant Lifestyle is not about being perfect or attaining perfection. There are no unicorns and rainbows here. A radiant life and lifestyle are perfectly imperfect! With grace, you face the challenges that come your way. You take time to look behind the challenge and see the gift for your growth. You use this time to let go of your old self and bring out more of your authentic self. And when you realize you are off course, you gently realign with the powers, committing again to live a radiant lifestyle.

A woman's Radiance is fully expressed when she wholeheartedly loves herself, puts her gifts and talents into action, and passionately pursues the callings of her soul.

Living a Radiant Lifestyle, you see yourself as the co-creator of your life. Tapping in to your calling, desires, dreams, and visions inspires your action to bring them to life. Your actions will not be self-sacrificing. Rather they will rise from a loving and compassionate perspective, one that honors who you are and where you uniquely desire to go. Living a Radiant Lifestyle, you will feel more natural and at ease, and answers, help, and opportunities will magically flow your way. That magic is the Universe, God, or your higher power stepping in to bring to life your desires. Living a Radiant Lifestyle shifts your inner world. You feel different about yourself, more love toward yourself and more gratitude for your uniqueness and the gifts you bring to the world. The inner shift translates into an outer shift, too. You see yourself differently. When you look in the mirror, you refrain from critical comments. Instead, you look lovingly into your eyes and see your true beauty. You see a Radiance and glow that you haven't seen in a long time, maybe ever. Your Radiance and glow become palpable.

As you extend your Radiance into the world, your interactions with family, friends, co-workers and the community begin to shift. People notice a change about you, even if they can't put their finger on it. Expect feedback about your incredible energy. Frequently I hear, "I love your energy," and it lights me up to know that I am living in alignment with my authentic self. People will be magnetically drawn to you. You will be visible in ways you never imagined. As you journey through your radiant life in this deeply connected way, you understand more clearly that your life matters, and you feel this truth from your interactions with people. Your relationships become richer. Your conversations are deeper, more intimate. You will easily share more vulnerably about your life and dreams with those closest to you, your inner circle. You will connect with others who are also committed to living radiantly.

Your view of the world expands when you decide to live a Radiant Lifestyle. You open yourself to see and understand empowering and timeless life principles. You no longer see yourself as only in physical form. You see yourself as a spiritual being first and foremost. As you continue to surrender to the guidance of your inner wisdom and your higher power, you find a new joy. You become more curious and playful. Your energy isn't absorbed by the old paradigm of strategy and control, so you have the space to imagine and discover the deeper callings of your soul. Radiant living requires you to continue to grow and expand into the fullest version of you!

You are a beautiful flower blossoming into your authentic Radiance.

I like to think of radiant living this way: Imagine you are a gorgeous rose plant, like one of the gold-medal winners at a flower show. You have multiple blooms, and each bloom has hundreds of petals. Before you show the Radiance of your fully expressed flowers, you have some work to do—you need to grow! For you, that might be to grow into your worth, to grow your connection to your inner voice and intuition, or to grow your ability to take inspired action. All these powers help you to grow into your fullest beauty.

To blossom, you will need to break out of the outer shell that protects your petals. The shell represents your protective ego, but your inner self senses that an amazing, beautiful, powerful woman is wrapped tightly within her ego. You have fed yourself with your self-worth and with your mindset, you've connected to your calling, and you are ready to take inspired action to blossom! It is time to bring the gift of you to the world. You begin to open beyond the safety of your tight buds. Opening exposes you to rain, wind, cold temperatures, and even little gnats that threaten the fullest opening of your blooms. But you persevere, because this natural unfolding can't be stopped. You are committed to being fully you in the world. You do your best to stand tall and face the obstacles. You can't retreat into the bud; your blooms continue to open, little by little, with deeper and deeper trust in yourself, knowing God would not have given you the desire to bloom if you didn't have the capability to do so.

You continue on, day after day, bit by bit. Warm sunshine fuels you, and you grow faster. Dark stormy days cause you to hunker down and weather the storm. You take note of how beautiful you are each day. You marvel in what is unfolding, as you had no idea how radiant you could be by simply being authentically you. A weed may hold you back, but the gardener comes, carefully bends down and examines the weed. She gently places her hands at the base of the weed, close to your precious trunk, and pulls the weed out. Your trunk moves a little bit, and you feel the ground around you shift, but when the dirt settles, you have more room to grow. What seemed like a safe fellow plant had actually been blocking your growth. This cycle continues, and then one miraculous day you are in full bloom! Your full Radiance is there for all to see. You have arrived. You glow from the inside out. You have achieved in this season what you came here to do.

Next year, you start all over again! When you step into the best version you and you express that in the world, you set yourself up to grow bigger, stronger, and more radiant. Year after year the cycle continues; your growth and unfolding are without end. Just when you think you've reached your fullest potential, your gardener feeds and fertilizes you, and you willingly soak it deep into your roots. Your radiant potential expands. You are like the beautiful, fully blossoming rose bush. You have touched many lives: the gardener who smiled each time she tended to you, the passersby who marveled at your beauty year after year, and the people who held bouquets of your blooms. Recognize your blossoms and put them into action in your life!

A Radiant Lifestyle naturally unfolds when you
engage the Powers of Radiant Achievement.

To engage, embody, and live a Radiant Lifestyle, you will take on new beliefs and ways of being. Each one of these shifts supports you to live your fullest, most joyful, and turned-on life. Here's how it looks to live each of the Powers of Radiant Achievement:

1. **You own your SELF-WORTH.**
   - You know you are enough, regardless of what you have or have not achieved.
   - You have no need to prove yourself to gain self-worth.
   - You realize you don't have all the answers, but that doesn't stop you from being self-confident.
   - You see and appreciate your unique gifts to the world, and you put your skills into action.
   - You do not judge yourself or others.
   - You don't need anyone's permission to follow your dreams or listen to your intuition.
   - You follow your dreams, even if you haven't figured it all out, because you trust there is a higher reason for your dreams.
   - You know you owe it to yourself to pursue your passions.

2. **You have an empowered MINDSET.**

   - You are conscious of your self-talk and take steps to eliminate the thoughts and beliefs that hold you back from being your best self.

   - You see the stories that shaped you into who you are today, and you willingly let the old stories go and craft empowered stories to support creation of the life you dream of.

   - You don't accept *this is who I am,* because you know you continually transform as you transform your thoughts.

   - You not only have empowering thoughts and beliefs about yourself, you also see others and the world through a lens of hope and possibility.

   - You live in the present moment, and you see time as a gift.

3. **You have developed your Power of INNER LISTENING.**

   - You take time every day to connect with your higher self.

   - You hear what your intuition is telling you, and you honor the messages.

   - You know that listening is as important as thinking to achieve your goals.

   - You use curiosity and wonder to connect with your intuition.

   - You welcome the guidance from your intuition and trust what you hear.

   - You live from this place of listening; as a result, you experience a state of flow, where things magically unfold for you.

   - You don't worry about things, because you know that whatever is happening in your world will help you grow and be polished into a more alive and authentic version of yourself.

4. **You make a habit of taking INSPIRED ACTION.**
   - You live your life with a beautiful blend of listening and action.
   - You take your next best action, inspired by your higher self or by a serendipitous divine message from a friend, phone call, or email.
   - Next steps and new opportunities come to you frequently, and you recognize the gifts and act on them.
   - You believe things can be easy and that you will work toward your goal, but instead of struggle and strife, your path is one of inspiration and flow.
   - By connection with the inspiration, you can feel when it's time to think strategically and, at the same time, to be open and receptive to better answers and solutions.

5. **You have a strong COMMITMENT to yourself and your goals and dreams.**
   - You are deeply connected to what your heart is calling you to do, even if it doesn't make logical sense.
   - You walk with openness and trust, knowing that when the time is right, your dream will manifest.
   - Your commitment is to be open to do what it takes to move toward your goal, to step into the unknown, to face your fears, to be a beginner, even if you've been an expert for many years.
   - You are committed to the journey, even if you take some detours on the way.
   - You don't have to know exactly how or when it will unfold, and you do not have to know what the final result will be.

6. **You use REFLECTION to more deeply appreciate your life and your journey.**
   - You consistently spend time to gauge the flow of every aspect of your life.

- You look for lessons learned, not from a place of judgment, but from a place of empowerment and growth.
- You take time to acknowledge and appreciate the steps you have taken, the fears you have overcome, and the stories you have rewritten.
- You are deeply in tune with life around you.
- You see and appreciate the ways your path unfolds with grace and ease.
- You express gratitude often for the small and large blessings in your life.

7. **You use RITUAL to add mindfulness and sacredness to your life.**
   - You are in touch with your desires, likes, and preferences.
   - You know what activities help center you, and you engage in them on a regular basis.
   - You know what connects you to nature, what brings you peace, and what energizes you.
   - You balance your day with work time, listening time, play time, and time for rituals.
   - You see rituals as small, sacred moments that feel peaceful in all circumstances.
   - Your rituals keep you grounded and focused, despite what obstacles come your way.

Take one step TODAY to live a Radiant Lifestyle.

Are you ready to live a Radiant Lifestyle, or are you hesitant? A Radiant Lifestyle might seem difficult or impossible at first. Maybe you see yourself as too old, too set in your ways, too afraid, too busy, or this doesn't seem like your "thing." I hear you and honor your concern and belief. At the same time, I will say this thinking is not the real you. Those stories and excuses come from your ego, not from your true essence. It makes sense that you are hearing these stories. It's how your ego tries to keep you safe. Unfortunately, staying safe can restrict you from following your callings and desires and living your most radiant life. Remind yourself why you picked up this book. Is there a yearning inside of you to let your Radiance shine? Connect to that yearning and watch your ego and objections subside. Stand strong with me as I support you to begin your journey, with baby steps if needed. Baby steps will begin a beautiful unfolding of your innate Radiance!

To change your life and live a Radiant Lifestyle, you must do one thing: You must draw a line in the sand and COMMIT to be open to living differently from what you have been doing. One simple, powerful commitment is your first step toward living a Radiant Lifestyle, and you can do it right now, right here. Speak this statement out loud (do it in a mirror for even greater impact), feeling your commitment in your body.

Today, right here and now, I am drawing a line in the sand.
I am committing to living my life from a new perspective.
I am committed to learning and embodying the Powers of
Radiant Achievement and living a Radiant Lifestyle.

Fantastic! You have taken one big, empowered step for your future. Armed with this commitment, begin your journey with wonder and curiosity. The beginning shifts may feel strange, different, and even uncomfortable. That's to be expected, as you face and will shift from stories, habits, and beliefs that you've carried for decades. Hang in there. Know that things will unfold exactly as they are meant to unfold. There is no right or wrong way to go about this. Stay connected to your inner voice, and your magical journey will take you to places you've never imagined. In the next chapter, you will learn practical steps to integrate this new paradigm into your life.

A Pause for Reflection: Understanding Your
Embodiment of a Radiant Lifestyle

In this reflection, you will pause to explore your own experience and embodiment of a Radiant Lifestyle. Grab your journal. Find a quiet place to sit and listen without interruption. Take a couple of deep breaths to get centered and to connect with your inner wisdom. When you are ready, write your responses to the following questions:

1. *In what ways am I already living a Radiant Lifestyle?*

2. *In what ways have I been limiting myself from living a Radiant Lifestyle?*

3. *What next steps can I take to more consciously live a Radiant Lifestyle?*

BONUS MATERIAL

Enter "800014" in the Radiant Achiever APP TRACK NOW page to unlock additional content related to this chapter.

CHAPTER 12

Integrating the Powers Into Your Life

Integrating and embodying the Powers of Radiant Achievement takes you out of frenzy and turns on your life, your essence, and your soul-centered calling.

Congratulations for taking this journey to awaken your Radiance! By consciously reading this book and participating in the end-of-chapter activities and reflection questions, you have officially activated your Powers of Radiant Achievement. You have taken a bold, empowered, and courageous step.

In Part 2 of this book you connected with and reflected on seven core superpowers that you possess, including:

POWER 1: THE POWER OF AUTHENTIC SELF-WORTH

- You are enough always and in all ways.
- Self-worth is about confidence, self-love, and owning who YOU are.

POWER 2: THE POWER OF MINDSET

- Your mindset is driving you, whether you are aware of it or not.
- Your mindset shapes your actions, which creates your results.

POWER 3: THE POWER OF INNER LISTENING

- You can feel and hear what your inner (higher) self is saying and feeling.
- Inner listening connects to your intuition, your creativity, and your potential.

POWER 4: THE POWER OF INSPIRED ACTION

- You can take the next best step from a place of trust, without attachment to the outcome.
- Inspired action brings joy, creativity, and wonder to life and opens you up to receive support from the Universe.

POWER 5: THE POWER OF COMMITMENT

- You know to commit to what your soul desires, not necessarily what your mind wants, and to be unattached to the timing of manifestation.
- The commitment to achieve is the quiet perseverance you maintain from a place of deep trust and knowing.

POWER 6: THE POWER OF REFLECTION

- You easily get quiet to listen and feel the results of a situation, to see and celebrate the baby steps, to feel grateful for the journey.
- Reflection keeps you fueled for the journey and keeps you in awareness and growth.

POWER 7: THE POWER OF RITUAL

- You look at your life and your daily routines with an element of mindfulness and sacredness.
- Ritual brings deeper peace and gratitude to your life.

Additionally, you learned what it takes to be a Radiant Leader and live a Radiant Lifestyle. So now what? Where do you go from here? Let me suggest a simple path to start leading, living, and being your most radiant and turned-on self using the Powers of Radiant Achievement as a new paradigm and guide. The following five key steps will support you to absorb your most important lessons from this book and to begin transforming to the life you desire.

STEP 1: Do an inner assessment on the learnings from the book.

This book sets out ideas, concepts, tools, and practices. Some may feel easy and natural for you; others may feel less useful. That is to be expected, as we are each unique, and we each come from different places and different perspectives. A smooth transition to a life of Radiant Achievement requires preparation. One of the best ways to prepare for your journey is to perform an inner assessment.

An inner assessment is a check-in and connection with what you are feeling and experiencing about what you have learned in this book. Use a journal to capture your answers to the following questions:

A. How am I feeling about me and my Radiance?
B. What inner shifts have I noticed about me and my life?
C. What outer shifts have I noticed?
D. What do I feel when I look in the mirror? Do I see someone different? Do I see myself differently? Can I see and feel more of my authentic beauty and Radiance?

E. Review your notes from the chapter reflections and ask: What new insights came up for me at the end of each chapter?

F. What powers do I realize I am already using?

G. What powers resonate most with me and what powers am I avoiding?

Your insights will help you assess more fully how to integrate the Powers of Radiant Achievement. While it's good to have knowledge (like you now do), I firmly believe that knowledge without action is wasted. I thank Stephen Covey for my deep commitment to implement at least one change in my life from every book I read. I'd love for you to do the same from the information presented to you here.

STEP 2: Complete the Powers of Radiant Achievement Self-Assessment.

In this step, you will complete a self-assessment on the Powers of Radiant Achievement. I call it the Ring of Radiance. The assessment helps you to "see" your Radiance. Your degree of Radiance is a baseline to use as you further integrate, apply, and embody the powers. Please set aside some quiet, uninterrupted time for this exercise. Give yourself at least an hour, more if you have a lot to say or if you love to color! When you are ready, follow the instructions included with the assessment diagram. My clients do these same actions as part of my signature programs to gain clarity about where they are, what's most important to them, and what next steps are key for them now. This process will help you discover key ways to put this material to deeper use to transform your life.

Ring of Radiance Self-Assessment

A. **Assess your use and embodiment of the Powers of Radiant Achievement**

Instructions: On a scale of 1-10, how activated is each power in your life? Put a dot on each line to represent how strong that power is NOW. Connect the dots and color the lined in area yellow for a visual representation of your embodiment.

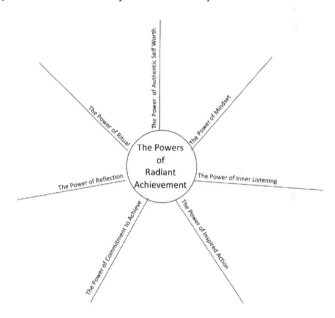

B. **Reflect on your results using the following questions:**
- How wide is my Radiance?
- What power(s) are most active for me? Give one or two examples how this power has played out in my life.

- What power(s) need further activation? What negative impact am I experiencing because this power is missing or less used?
- What do I see is possible for me? What are some ways I can expand my powers?

C. **Decide your next steps to further activate your Powers of Radiant Achievement.**
   - What power(s) am I feeling the need to address and expand right now, and why?
   - What goals or dreams am I working toward (or can start working toward now) using these powers? Which specific power will I apply to which specific goal or dream?
   - What action(s) will I commit to for the next week to build each specific power?
   - Who will I share my commitment with to support me in my journey?

Please share your results and commitments
on my private Facebook group,
"The Radiant Achievement Inner Circle": www.facebook.
com/groups/theRadiantAchievementInnerCircle.

A couple key things to note about your work here: This assessment is based on a specific point in time. As you continue to expand your use of these powers, your assessment will change. I suggest you write the date at the top of the assessment that you take. In the future, you can look at your assessments and celebrate progress!

Another key thing is that you may see a decrease in one area as you step out in other areas. That is okay and not unusual. I recently did a new assessment for myself and I noticed that my Power of Reflection and Power of Ritual had shrunk. I inquired as to the cause and realized that when I was in highly inspired action, I was not engaging the other powers as consciously as I had been before.

I noticed my old habit of moving too fast, and I made some shifts of mindset to create more space for reflection and rituals. Now my sun is more balanced and radiant!

One final note about your assessment: The more connected you are to the potential of these powers, the tougher you may be grading yourself. That's okay too. The assessments are relative to your current place on your path, and they are not meant to judge or criticize. Each assessment offers information to help you connect with your needs to deepen one or more powers. The journey never ends, so enjoy the ride!

STEP 3: Implement your desired actions and next steps.

Acting on your next steps is a necessary and important part of your transformation into a life turned on. Here is where the rubber meets the road, as they say. Thoughts alone will not take you where you want to go. You must take action. Consider these questions as you take inspired and necessary action:

- What do I need to do to make space for inspired actions? What things do I need to stop doing? What things do I need to start doing?
- How will I schedule these steps into my day? Will I put them on my to-do list as a top priority?
- Do I want to share my actions with someone who will hold me accountable?

STEP 4: Support your integration and transformation by reciting the poem, "My Radiant Essence."

When I developed my workshop-retreat, "Radiance Awakened," I wrote a poem that we read out loud at the end of the workshop. The moment was transformational; we lifted our voices together with power and conviction. It helped to cement into our bodies each of the Powers of Radiant Achievement. It will be the perfect ending to our time together on this journey of activation and integration of your radiant powers.

I encourage you to recite this poem daily as a new ritual to support your integration of the Powers of Radiant Achievement. Each day speak these powerful mantras out loud. For added impact, do this ritual in front of a mirror and feel every word vibrate in your body. Like the Mindful Moment Radiance Ritual, this action will support your transformation to living your most radiant life!

MY RADIANT ESSENCE

Today I commit to awaken my Radiance, to pursue
my goals and desires using the powers of Radiant
Achievement, to lead where I am called to lead, and
to live my life as my most authentic, radiant self.
I see and own my worth.
I AM ENOUGH. I AM RADIANT.
I hear the thoughts I think and consciously choose
to adopt a mindset that uplifts and empowers.
I AM EMPOWERED. I AM RADIANT.
I listen to my soul, for it knows my truth, potential, and purpose.
I AM PRESENT AND OPEN. I AM RADIANT.
I take inspired action based on my intuition and inner knowing.
I AM COURAGEOUS. I AM RADIANT.
I commit to achieve my yearnings and desires in their perfect time.
I AM STEADFAST. I AM RADIANT.
I pause periodically to recognize, acknowledge, and
celebrate my accomplishments, growth, and learnings.
I AM GRATEFUL. I AM RADIANT.
I engage in rituals to connect and move me to my deeper
truth, to my radiant essence, and to my desires.
I AM GROUNDED. I AM RADIANT.

STEP 5: Join me in co-creating a new culture where living and leading with Radiance is the norm.

This book is coming to its end, but our journey together is only beginning! One of the most significant shifts and changes you can make is to connect and journey with other like-minded women. I invite you to join my tribe and journey with us. I am committed to create a new society where Radiant Achievement, Radiant Leadership, and a Radiant Lifestyle are the norm. Whether your calling is to lead a cause, start a company, facilitate a club, or simply to live a Radiant Lifestyle in your home or community, you are part of the unfolding of a NEW culture and society.

In this culture and society:

- women see, own, and appreciate their Radiance;
- women see their true beauty reflected through their being, love, compassion, and gifts;
- women define success by following their hearts to bring their gifts, talents, and passions into the world;
- all people KNOW their worth and have a deep connection to their potential to make a difference in the world;
- all people know that their life matters.

This is the world I desire to help create and live in! Join with me at http://www.christinemariehoward.com/ to co-create this new reality. On my website you can participate in a number of ways:

1. Sign up for my newsletter for inspiration and education, news and events, and powerful support to guide you on your journey as a Radiant Leader to live a turned-on Radiant Lifestyle.
2. Join one of my workshops to help you clarify your calling and vision.

CHRISTINE HOWARD

3. Join my mastermind to support you in bringing your calling to life.

In closing, please know that I see your Radiance, and I am taking a stand for you to see it and bring it to the world. I am humbled and honored to have shared my journey and the new paradigm of achievement—Radiant Achievement—with you. I look forward to journeying together!

A Pause for Reflection: Understanding Your
Life as a RADIANT ACHIEVER

In this reflection, you have the opportunity to look at your own experience and embodiment as a Radiant Achiever. Grab your journal. Find a quiet place to sit and listen without interruption. Take a couple of deep breaths to get centered and to connect with your inner wisdom. When you are ready, write your responses to the following questions:

1. *In what ways do I see myself as a Radiant Achiever?*

2. *In what ways have I been limiting or ignoring my powers as a Radiant Achiever?*

3. *What next steps can I take to more consciously step into and expand my ability to be a Radiant Achiever?*

BONUS MATERIAL

Enter "800015" in the Radiant Achiever APP TRACK NOW page to unlock additional content related to this chapter.

AFTERWORD

MINDFUL MOMENTS FOR RADIANCE

Being your most Radiant Self occurs in mindful moments.

In this book, you have read stories of my journey in reawakening my creativity, taking a stand to love myself authentically, and ultimately creating the Mantra Makeup Mat™ and the Mantra Mindset Moments brand of products.

Whether you want to lose weight, find a new job, or courageously pursue your soul-centered calling, the right tools and a positive environment will support your success. Have you ever cleaned out a pantry or refrigerator and then gone shopping for clean food before starting a health goal? Or have you bought new clothes in preparation for a new job?

The same mindful preparation applies to begin living a Radiant Life and pursuing your soul-centered calling. The Mantra Makeup Mat™ and Mantra Mindset Moments™ products can help you out. The mission of this brand is to support women's empowerment. We help 21st-century women to take mindful moments in their day to connect with their worth, own their uniqueness, and celebrate their individuality, so that they can live confidently and shine their brilliant beauty. Whether it be one of our wildly popular Mantra Makeup Mats™, one of our clever t-shirts, or the Mindful Moment Radiance Ritual card that we include with each product, having and using these tools daily will support your inner and outer transformation.

How many products do we purchase that have little or no value after the initial thrill wears off? The Mantra Mindset Moments products add more value each time you use them. Set up your environment for success by adding one of these highly inspirational, eco-friendly, made-in-the-USA products to your transformational toolkit and your home!

Visit us at www.mantramindsetmoments.com to explore our latest designs and to order your favorites. Enter "RAbook" for a single-use 10% discount on your first order.

COMPANY
CONTACT PAGE

"It's time for all women to fully connect with, see, and own
their radiant power and beauty.
Their soul needs this.
The world needs this!"
— Christine Howard

Email: Christine@ChristineMarieHoward.com
Mailing Address: 2683 Via de la Valle G-309, Del Mar, CA 92014
Phone: 858-367-0337
Website: http://www.christinemariehoward.com/

RESOURCES

Visit christinemariehoward.com for these additional resources:

- The Radiant Achiever APP
- Soul-Centered Fulfillment book
- Radiant Achievement Inspiration card
- Full line of Mantra Mindset Moments Products
- Current offerings for Coaching, Speaking, and Workshops

Recommended Reading:

- Becoming Supernatural by Dr. Joe Dispenza, https://www.hayhouse.com/becoming-supernatural-paperback
- Rise. Amazing Woman. Rise by Marsh Engle, https://www.theamazingwomannation.com/rise
- Soul Shifts by Dr. Barbara DeAngelis, https://www.hayhouse.com/soul-shifts-paperback
- The Big Leap by Gay Hendricks, https://www.amazon.com/Big-Leap-Conquer-Hidden-Level
- The Surrender Experiment by Michael Singer, https://untetheredsoul.com/surrender-experiment
- The Untethered Soul by Michael Singer, https://untetheredsoul.com/untethered-soul

Other Recommended Resources:

- Meditation: Insight Timer App, insighttimer.com
- Healing Music: Mark Romero, markromeromusic.com
- EFT/Tapping: Nick Ortner, thetappingsolution.com
- Biofeedback: Deepak Chari of the Chari Center of Health, charicenter.com

Printed in the United States
by Baker & Taylor Publisher Services